DIALOGUES DREAMS
DREAMS + DIALOGUES

DS(2)01 2015-2018
EDITED BY ELANTHA EVANS
WITH JASDEEP ATWAL, VERONICA CAPPELLI, JOSHUA RICKETTS, GADE SMITH AND GIA SAN TU
CONTRIBUTIONS BY SOUMYEN BANDYOPADHYAY, DUSAN DECERMIC, CLARE HAMMAN, ANDY LOWE, ANTHONY POWIS & LAYTON REID

STUDIO AS BOOK
NO. 05
SCHOOL OF ARCHITECTURE + CITIES
UNIVERSITY OF WESTMINSTER

DIALOGUES + DREAMS

DS(2)01 2015-2018
EDITED BY ELANTHA EVANS
WITH JASDEEP ATWAL, VERONICA CAPPELLI, JOSHUA RICKETTS, GADÉ SMITH AND GIA SAN TU
CONTRIBUTIONS BY SOUMYEN BANDYOPADHYAY, DUSAN DECERMIC, CLARE HAMMAN, ANDY LOWE, ANTHONY POWIS & LAYTON REID

STUDIO AS BOOK
NO. 05
SCHOOL OF ARCHITECTURE + CITIES
UNIVERSITY OF WESTMINSTER

Studio as Book is a new series of yearly publications that tender the extraordinary creative work undertaken in the School of Architecture + Cities design studios. The series includes undergraduate and graduate level work, and is intended to sit alongside the Open Exhibition and catalogue. Each book in the series covers the work of a single design studio over the course of at least two years. Its objectives are:

- To record, archive, and present the pedagogical programme and creative student outputs of a design studio
- To position the work of a design studio within a broader intellectual, scientific or aesthetic field
- To advance the design driven research being undertaken in the School's design studios
- To provide a reference for future iterations and variations of a design studio

Reducing the creative output of a multi-year design studio to a single volume, is no easy undertaking, and it is necessarily selective. At the same time, it provides a consistent, sure platform for the wide range of approaches to the discipline of teaching architectural design which characterise the school.

Each Studio as Book has been peer-reviewed on the basis of a proposal submitted by the studio's tutors to an editorial committee. In addition to studio briefs and student work, each book includes content that draws out the studio's research and pedagogical agenda. The format that this takes varies from book to book – reflective essays by tutors or past students, interviews, theoretical essays from parallel fields, and so forth. The Studio as Book Series will later be accompanied by a Studio Pamphlet Series for design studios of a shorter duration.

I wish to acknowledge the contribution of the following in bringing this project to fruition: Lindsay Bremner, Director of Research, who was the driving force behind the series, Mark Boyce, author of *Sizes May Vary: A workbook for graphic design* (Lawrence King, 2008) – and the designer of the preliminary template for Studio as Book, and Filip Visnjic, designer of the series' website:

http://www.studioasbook.org

Harry Charrington
Head of School of Architecture + Cities
University of Westminster

DIALOGUES + DREAMS

DIALOGUES + DREAMS

DS(2)01 2015-2018
EDITED BY ELANTHA EVANS
WITH JASDEEP ATWAL, VERONICA CAPPELLI, JOSHUA RICKETTS, GADE SMITH AND GIA SAN TU
CONTRIBUTIONS BY SOUMYEN BANDYOPADHYAY, DUSAN DECERMIC, CLARE HAMMAN, ANDY LOWE, ANTHONY POWIS & LAYTON REID

STUDIO AS BOOK
NO. 05
SCHOOL OF ARCHITECTURE + CITIES
UNIVERSITY OF WESTMINSTER

To David,
who taught without teaching

CONTENTS

This publication attempts to describe the layers of a world that existed for a defined period of time in the second year of the BA Architecture course at the University of Westminster, from September 2015 to June 2018. It explores the individual journeys that wended their way within it, the collective endeavour of the studio group, the studio's own progression year on year, and also my own wider journey through a deepening understanding of architecture education, its relevance and its possibilities. The intention is to show the work as it was at the time; not post-rationalised, not photo-shopped and not over-presented. Many 'final' drawings have been omitted. No project has been given more importance than the next. It is hoped that through the selection and combination of images for each, the relationship between thematic ambition, design development, media used, and architectural proposal becomes clear. The writings that sit either side of the central section containing the three years of studio work, are suggestive, reflective and hopefully thought-provoking; considering how and why we set up our design studios in the context of the university and architecture education. These pieces can be dipped in and out of, or read as a whole, together layering and progressing a line of questioning around the canons of architecture education and what the future might hold.

I believe that publishing a 'studio-as-book' from this non-degree-awarding year is significant in declaring and demonstrating that much can be gained in that interstitial year between arrival and graduation.

The dialogues and dreams of DS(2)01 – its students of architecture, architectural educators and practising architects – are here shared with you.

PROLOGUE
A THIRDSPACE IN TERTIARY PLACE?

INSIDE AS OUTSIDERS I

PART I : INSTITUTE BENJAMENTA
IN CONVERSATION WITH ANDY LOWE, 21 MARCH 2013

'Inside as Outsiders' was originally submitted as part of the MA in 'History & Critical Thinking' at the Architectural Association, which I completed in 2013. The opening discussion in the MA's 'debate series' was led by Andy Lowe, and entitled 'The Architectural Outside'. It acted as a trigger for this piece and was fundamental in opening up my approach to, understanding of, and communication about, architecture and design practices. This 'conversation' between myself and Andy Lowe considers the potential of how 'The Outside' could be used as a tool for conceptual understanding in the context of architecture education and its physical and perceived boundaries with both institutions and place. The introductions and conversation that follow are presented as originally submitted.

reference to literary conception, development and the demands that he sees literature placing on the attention of both author and reader. This notion had also been developed by Lefebvre and Foucault, and the three were connected by Etienne Balibar in his lecture at Central Saint Martin's in February 2013. Their idea of a thought 'from the outside' or the possibility of a 'pure outside', or the depersonalisation of the subject in order to create the 'uncanny double' or the 'neuter', could be one way to look back again, afresh, perhaps adding something to the binarised discourse that dominates architecture education and practice.

ANDY LOWE is a lecturer and architectural theorist within the Department of Visual Cultures and the Centre for Research Architecture at Goldsmiths College, London.

A SPECIFIC CONSIDERATION OF THE POTENTIAL OF HOW 'THE OUTSIDE' COULD BE USED AS A TOOL FOR CONCEPTUAL UNDERSTANDING IN THE CONTEXT OF ARCHITECTURE EDUCATION

Maurice Blanchot describes what could be called 'The Outside', 'An Other', or 'The Moment' in 'The Space of Literature', with particular

His main research interests are focused in the subject areas of Urban Cultures and Architectural Theory, the History of Art History, Modern

Art History, Cultural Studies and Cultural Theory. Andy studied at the University of Edinburgh and then at the Centre for Contemporary Studies at the University of Birmingham. Recent research has centred on a genealogy of formalism from the perspectives of technologies of the body and how these are intricate in the transformation of art and architectural histories and forms of criticism. These techniques range from the narrowly scientific to a wider view of the body as inscribed by virtual domains and currencies. At present the main focus of this research has concentrated on their spatial and configurative concerns as they apply to aspects of the architectural experience.

ELANTHA EVANS is an architect and architecture educator, predominantly teaching Design Studio at the University of Bath but also actively involved with RIBA Validation Panels in the UK and Overseas. Before setting up an Architecture Studio with Ana Serrano – Serrano Evans Partnership – Elantha worked with Richard Rogers Partnership on a variety of projects including Madrid-Barajas Airport, with Tim Ronalds on Hackney Empire Theatre and with Evans & Shalev Architects. Current practice work brings together architecture, interior and object design and is occasionally balanced with the production of site-specific performances and installations. Early on, from 2000-2002, practice work was punctuated with a two year stint at the University of Hong Kong as a Design Tutor and Senior Research Assistant. Elantha

is now working towards an MA in History & Critical Thinking at the Architectural Association, of which this submission forms a part.

THIS INTERVIEW took place on 21 March 2013 at Goldsmiths College. It was recorded with the permission of Andy Lowe and then transcribed and edited by Elantha Evans.

EE *Perhaps to begin, we could reflect upon some of the boundaries, internal contradictions and driving forces that we have both experienced first-hand in our roles within academia and in the context of the apparent impasse through the binary discourse that exists between science and art, or design and technology? And then later, we will move on to attempt to elucidate how the idea of 'an outside' or a 'third place', another space, could be useful as a conceptual, or intellectual tool, to try to reconsider the perceived place of architectural education within its systems of operation.*

AL Ok, so if you are looking at the kind of threshold between practice and knowledge, and the academisation of architecture, then that has a set of conceptual shifts that are marked by a different network of institutions, so almost by beginning by placing it within the University, I think you miss out the ways in which those thresholds shift. In one sense, up to about the middle of the eighteenth century, everyone learnt architecture – the trivium and the quadrivium – which was the basis for the late Hellenic education system; it was really the kind of basis for what you might say was a model of liberal education. The trivium was the first part: poetics, rhetoric and dialectics. Then the quadrivium, which was all based on mathematical ideas of knowledge; so you learnt arithmetic, geometry, music and architecture; there are a number of variants, such as astronomy, in the combination. In good Pythagorean style they are all conceived within that mathematical notion. You might see then a way in which the threshold between practice and knowledge or theory moves around in different kind of frameworks; re-conceived and re-conceived. A whole academic repertoire later begins to be built around that notion of the 'idea' and it resurfaces in different contexts and forms. One of the crucial things is, as you say, the way in which a notion that constitutes an 'idea' in the liberal arts gets split from the crafts – as being below that level of the 'idea'. 'Fine Arts' and the 'Academies' spring from this and so there is already an organised transformation of the model of education into a set of standardised academies, the chief of those is the 'École des Beaux Arts' which had this key architecture school stuck in there. That then survives into the 1960s and it is one of the keys ways in which the Arts were recognised as a distinct pursuit.

EE *I realised yesterday that between us, we are professionally involved in quite an interesting triad of universities: Goldsmiths, the Architectural Association (AA) and the University of Bath. Goldsmiths, where we are sitting today, is described as a Department of Art within the University of London, but as I understand it, was founded as a 'Technical and Recreative Institute'. The AA tries to maintain a position as far outside of institutional bodies as it can feasibly stay, whilst continuing to operate and be validated as an independent architecture school. Then there is Bath, where the Department of Architecture sits inside a Faculty of Engineering and within a University that has no Arts Faculties at all. So, there we have three very different situations. Whilst Bath is driven with a technological lean, emphasis on the understanding of making, and ruled quite heavily by the immobility and bureaucracy of 'University as Institution', there is still a push from certain parts of the school and from particular tutors to strive for the 'idea', or the 'vision' in a project; for freedom if you like. Then you have the AA which is driven by ideas and imagination and cutting edge technologies; pushing to the future, to what we do not already know, to what we think we don't already know – then that is pulled towards making and buildability, and in some ways is pulled towards a more bureaucratic tick-box approach than is in its nature. Presumably Goldsmiths brings another set of relationships to the table, both as an Art Department within a large university conglomeration, and also more specifically, with the Centre for Research Architecture which sits within the Visual Cultures Department. Then, in terms of teaching, both you and I are 'outsiders' working as part-time tutors on the 'inside' of these Institutions. In the context of your contribution to the AA HCT Debate*

Series – with 'The Architectural Outside' – this idea very much interested me and triggered me to write a short research proposal entitled 'Inside as an Outsider', which you have kindly read in advance of this conversation. My proposal also introduces the relevance of searching for "the appearance and loss, or transformation of the 'idea', its understanding and presentation; of academia or scholarship within universities and the interdependencies or relationships that exist with practice, policy, research and teaching."

AL Actually I also studied in Edinburgh, between the University and the Arts School, which is yet another situation; the Art College had its own Architecture Department which was affiliated to Herriot Watt and we had a big department of architecture in the University of Edinburgh. The Art Department itself was connected to the University and not to Herriot Watt, because that was Engineering. There was enormous rivalry and interest between the two. I went to the University and the Arts School – it was a joint degree across the two institutions which also had its own difficulties – I did Art History and

University, making one Department of Architecture; homogenised on paper and just about co-existing I think, in reality.

AL In a state of continuous warfare now... Then it was also difficult, the University thought it might be helpful to learn a few techniques and the Art college thought we were wasting our time reading books. This is a caricature, of course. It was about a half an hour walk between the two, and it felt as wide as the whole world! Most of the people I knew were in the Architecture School and there were always a lot of very interesting conversations going round, but it was on that kind of informal level.

EE *I am sure it wasn't in a space designed with that intent? But rather facilitated through the interdisciplinary environment?*

AL Exactly, not at all. All my work was really centred at those points of cross-disciplinary interactions, so not only starting off between those two very different institutions in Edinburgh, I next went to the Centre for Contemporary Culture Studies

> THERE HAS TO BE SOME KIND OF OPENING, THERE HAS TO BE SOME KIND OF ROOM FOR MANOEUVRE, WHERE YOU CAN PURSUE QUESTIONS

the Philosophy of Art at the University and drawing and painting at the Art School.

EE *How nice! And then recently the Art School was forced to merge with the*

in Birmingham, which again was deliberately set up as a crossing point between three or four disciplines, in order that new kinds of modes of research could be explored. In one sense, from that place a whole

Cultural Studies industry has evolved. At the time new modes often have very limited effects within the host institutions. They almost react by drawing back behind their boundaries, but it does create opportunities, creates spaces in which, practices that then kind of made it a place where new things were talked about that undid the core focus of teacher training. People began to... well one of the first results is the Department of Art, that then becomes the public face of the college. It had

VARIOUS AREAS OF TEACHING WERE BROUGHT INTO A COLLEGE, THAT DIDN'T HAVE A KIND OF SET AGENDA ABOUT WHAT YOUR OBJECTIVES WERE. THEY WERE GIVEN ROOM TO DEVELOP VERY DIFFERENTLY

exactly where you started, there has to be some kind of opening, there has to be some kind of room for manoeuvre, where you can pursue questions. In an odd way Goldsmiths developed in an odd way too, a distinct way, as for a lot of its life it was a Teacher Training Institute.

EE *Which looking at the prospectus, still comes through. And do you think that that is perhaps an example of one of those rare new ideas for a new way of testing inter-relations specifically, rather than infinite numbers with no guidance, that you say put four things together, that that has had interesting, positive outcomes?*

AL   Yes, yes. And in a kind of moment of consolidation – art schools and polytechnics have all been consolidated – it began to draw into it different kinds of smaller colleges. So in fact Goldsmiths' Department of Art came from another institution and its resources and studios. It eventually just assimilated a different set of

suddenly transformed itself into a 'liberal arts college'.

EE *And the philosophy of how one practices and learns here? The idea of a more hands-off, almost 'non-teaching' approach is fascinating. How much do you think that stems from its location and is not so much about old crafts and teaching painting?*

AL   I only wish I had been taught like that! I think you can put it down to various key figures in one way, but also I think, as a subtext, that various areas of teaching were brought into a college that didn't have a kind of set agenda about what your objectives were. They were given room to develop very differently. So there's room in the Theatre Department and the Department of Art and Music and so on, where they have been able to forge different kinds of possibilities in that kind of space. It is very interesting in an odd way that most of this happened when Richard Hoggart was the warden – he started the Centre for Contemporary Culture Studies. I almost think there was a lingering way, with this sense of a different way of trying to enquire into something that it initiated, though he had done that very much within and with English Literature. It really opened...and things really started to appear then.

EE *So what happens then when essentially Goldsmiths and say also Bath to a certain extent, have now built up an image based on their quite unique positions and identities? Are they then slaves to their own image? I don't know about Goldsmiths, but certainly the other two. So then, is that some sort of cycle of death? Is that idea of change*

AL I think the simplest answer would be to say 'crisis'! With the whole shift in the basis of funding and how research is funded. Every kind of institution is having to find its own position within that. The AA is not so constrained by that, but in one way Goldsmiths has reacted in a very similar way. We are a leading, research-based liberal arts college. We can't get out of that, we have to go for that route, so we cannot go back to some kind of traditional model, where we would teach traditionally these core disciplines. We can't do that. And whether that has an effect of having to negotiate a set of constant crises that shape relationships between departments because again,

IN FACT THEY HAD BEEN DESIGNED IN THE FIRST PLACE AS LOCAL H.E. INSTITUTES AND THEY WERE SUPPOSED TO HAVE A VERY STRONG RELATIONSHIP WITH THEIR LOCALITY, WITH LOCAL INDUSTRIES

and ambition to move forward, anew, going to stop and become very rigid, and then be put to one side? Or do you think there is a way through that?

AL Don't rock the boat!

EE *And in fact the AA has a similar situation, as I think there are people within it pushing conversations and debates, that are not what is necessarily publicised as being very 'AA' – but actually they are asking really pertinent questions, but they are doing that 'inside', but are almost too scared to admit to the outside, that this is what they are doing.*

departments which are succeeding in generating student income are going to be the lead departments and others which don't do that will tend to go into a cycle of losing out all the time; the more they lose, the less they will recruit. I really don't quite know.

EE *And do you think that the introduction of tuition fees levels the table at all, or will it exacerbate the problem?*

AL I think it is going to exacerbate the problem, I really do. As you say, institutions now are going to look for a clearer identity.

EE *Which might help the ones that have no identity, but I think it may stifle ones that have historically had an identity.*

AL Yes, I think some are retreating very quickly as you say, to a kind of stasis of 'this is what we are and this is what we do', others are finding it very difficult to negotiate that kind of identity in relationship to a student recruitment base. Places like east London I think are very badly placed because they built themselves around the idea of quite a big local catchment student body. These are students that are not going to be able to move miles away from home.

EE *And now they are not going to be able to go because they are not going to be able to afford it either.*

AL Exactly. There are a number like that around London, but I think it has hit east London very hard, so what

EE *Many new institutions want to use a School of Architecture as a flagship, with little idea as to what architectural education entails. It is curious that this is the case, even though there is little work in architecture at the moment. How can it still be a lure?*

AL I think there is a very obvious link to the demand for impact measures. Architecture offers a very explicit sense of impact, the trouble is that there is bugger all of it going on.

EE *No, nothing. Exactly.*

AL Then equally, it could also quickly drop off the agenda. If you think, one of the first signs of this was Cambridge, when it wanted to axe its Architecture Department as it didn't figure on their Research Profile. And then look at the old polytechnics and how they were turned into universities – there was a lot of

A LOT OF INTERESTING WORK, AND OFTEN BETTER RESEARCH WAS GOING ON IN THE POLYTECHNICS. THOSE KINDS OF NEW UNIVERSITIES WERE PUSHED INTO UNIVERSITY STATUS AS A POLITICAL MOVE

type of identity do they forge? It cannot be a 'community university' because it is not going to exist. They are going to be continuously pressed. So, do they make the most of their hardware to identify themselves? Trying to find one key lead discipline or something that will be linked to that. 'Here we are on the edge of London City Airport'...

interesting work, and often better research going on in the polytechnics. Those kinds of new universities were I think pushed into university status as a political move, to raise the profile of Higher Education in general, but many of them were circumscribed by their student intake. In fact they had been designed in the first place as local HE Institutes and they were supposed to have a very strong relationship with their locality, with local industries, for example the car industry in Coventry. That set up had produced a lot of interesting work, a lot of important work, then all of a sudden that is limited by how much research funding can you get from a new set of central institutions. How do you get your research recognised if it is no longer attached immediately to a particular set of interests or connections?

EE *It also homogenised everything. Whereas before you had a dialogue between the two different approaches of universities and polytechnics.*

AL And then, in addition, you often had a situation where people would come to a polytechnic from a university because something was going on there that you couldn't get access to with a traditional university format, and a lot of that also worked around the way in which art schools, architecture schools were caught up in slightly different versions across the place. There is a crucial point where you might say that the constructional architecture of a place and an organisational architecture of systems meet. Really at this point now, we cannot divide the two. And whether this is from the point of view of a pedagogy or a process of research on the thresholds of different kinds of academic institutions; or, if you like, deep in the kind of sets of operations that mark the relationship of the university to now, with the idea of an innovation-based economy; everything tied together. The shift

of universities from a Department of Education into a Department of Business and Skills, which was the work of Peter Mandelson, is, I think, a crucial step in reorienting the kinds of work and the kinds of operations that the universities will be involved in. So, in one sense, universities have, if you like, an overt organisational architecture; they are also intricated in much more extensive and developing ones. I think the one area where we can see our work opening is in the different ways in which those transactions are open to analysis and scrutiny, say exploring and testing borders like what the Forensic Architecture Project in the Centre of Research Architecture has done.

EE *What we are teaching and discussing in design schools has actually got little to do with what is going on in the world and so does one carry on structuring education to support our romantic notion of architecture? Or does one give in to what it has become and forget the rest? Perhaps that question can be easier transposed to the context of an Art School, like Goldsmiths, as a starting point?*

AL If you start with that sense of anachronism, that one of the key thresholds is always that anachronistic shift. Where does that begin to play? You can do interesting things with that. It is not 'now you have learnt to be an architect, here is the real situation', but there are key moments when it feels exactly like that.

EE *That is essentially what happens. In a way it has to happen. Otherwise you cannot get there. You have to pretend, you have to be not quite in the real world in order to learn and imagine.*

AL Indeed, if you pose the same question to Departments of Art, they will say – 'We are educating you for what? To become artists? Well the likelihood of even 5% of you to become full time artists who can live from your work is idealistic, so what are we doing?' Again you have the same sense that you are working with a demand. A lot of notions of creativity are being floated around; that we need the creative industries and so on... is becoming a kind of heavy profile. It would be an enormous

touched seemed romantic or if you can see their recapitulation into a very much more organisational set of demands. That challenges the notion of the creative, we are then in a sense stuck, really at a point where we are seeing something chopped off at the knees. Now, what is going to survive? What is the core of that notion of an unspoken demand? Where is that set of possibilities going to go? Nowhere, as far as we can see.

EE *At the moment?*

AL At the moment.

EE *But if it is lost completely now, it will never come back. It is going already.*

SHALL WE TEACH ARCHITECTURE STUDENTS THE REALITIES OF GLOBAL BUILDING JUST BECAUSE THE CHANCES ARE THAT IS WHERE THEY WILL END UP? YOU ARE HERE, BUT YOU ARE BEING EDUCATED FOR A PROFESSION THAT NO LONGER EXISTS

loss if an opportunity for such kinds of explorations vanishes. I am old enough now to think back a long time to when most working class kids had very little chance of getting anywhere near a Grammar School, and for kids with ideas, with talent, with imagination, Art School was a way of moving up and out.

EE *But now it is not going to be.*

AL No, and if you think of what that offered, whether the ideas you

AL What I mean is, shall we teach architecture students the realities of global building just because the chances are that is where they will end up? To train them for office duties? To give in to that? 'Actually you are here, but you are being educated for a profession that no longer exists. And what you will be called upon to do is garage extensions, conversions or catalogue selection or book of details'. And yet, if we pander to that through a 'reluctant realism', which is 'well we have to do that', then you would have to say there is no sense of you being here. But, inside that sense of reluctance we are still, in whatever way, paying court to that sense of possibility; so the thing is where do we focus, how do we get a grasp on it, otherwise in itself it becomes a rather staid anachronism and then we don't know what to do with it. So, this place that you are searching for in your research project is a place that keeps something open and keeps moving and these have got to be the only real places where we can begin to think about the 'idea'.

EE *That is the other place that I am trying to find, yes. Maybe that is it? The spaces that these schools do still enable.*

AL If you like, yes.

EE *No because it would probably kill it.*

AL Yes, you are right. So it is the institution and the individual. People work through the system, it is what makes it porous and the opposition if you like between institution and individual is not really the issue, it is the something that happens in-between.

EE *It is what happens on the general level which is harder, because we get excited about the things that are momentary, or relate to a particular person, subject or conversation. But the systemic mess is the general relationship. I suppose, the question is*

IT IS ALL OF THE KINDS OF THINGS THAT YOU CAN'T WRITE INTO A CURRICULUM

AL It is all of the kinds of things that you can't write into a curriculum.

EE *And it seems to be individuals who often counteract this systemic impasse with the perseverance of idea and reflection. So, can you ever get anywhere new or freer in terms of institutions generally, because actually you are just relying on the brain and energy of an individual, or at most a few interconnected individuals?*

AL So, do you think you could ever make it institutional or systemic?

EE *This 'thing', the 'other', the 'space' for ideas?*

how can one apply that way of thinking to help change the banality of the general inter-relations between things? Can one? And is anyone interested? Actually, it doesn't really benefit anyone in the system to consider this change. Is that a problem? Or like you say, if you try to institutionalise the 'idea' that we are discussing, maybe that is the end of it.

AL In a kind of way, it places us within the terms that we are hedging around, which is in the consideration of the different versions of 'the Outside'. It is perhaps the wrong place to have a theoretical argument, but yet it is the very thing that enables something to emerge – there is a very distinct difference between the 'Third Space' and the notion of an 'Outside', and what takes Blanchot through people like Foucault and so on, is different again. In a way, it is all a kind of refusal to submit to a set of categorical distinctions, organisations and institutionalisations. But it was an opening that in itself you cannot do anything with. It all ought to belong to each other, a sense of everything being lived on the ground, all the kinds of distinctions are temporary, they are always moving in and out of each other. That is fine, but, where do you go with that? Where can that kind of thinking spark something else? I found in Blanchot's direction, that sense of 'is it possible to think of an experience without a subject, outside the confines or limits of a subject?' very much more interesting. It takes you into that world of Foucault

how he presents his work in the early years which people tend to forget in the shape of the lectures that later come out of the 'College de France'. His sense that 'in every book I write I don't want to be the same person I was before during or after'.

EE *That is surely the same as a design project should be?*

AL Yes yes. There is here an interesting inverse in the novel by Robert Walser – *The Institute Benjamenta* – about a school for servants. The basis of it is that nobody seems to learn anything except that there are a whole series of precepts and rules and you memorise these and you rehearse them and you rehearse a whole series of movements. Now, one of the kind of rules is that the rules have already thought of everything.

ONE OF THE KIND OF RULES IS THAT THE RULES HAVE ALREADY THOUGHT OF EVERYTHING... A WORLD OF INFINITE REPETITION AND REHEARSAL... WHEN EVERYTHING HAS BEEN THOUGHT OF, THE ONLY THOUGHT IS 'OTHERWISE'

and gives you an immediate view of bodies of knowledge being shaped or formed, not as a structure but through that question of what relations can be established between them, and what is contained and what is done within them. I think of the beginning of *The Birth of the Clinic* by Foucault, written very close to the time when he wrote *The Thought of Outside*. There is a poetic about his early work and

All you are caught up in is a world of infinite repetition and rehearsal. In an institutionalised world of infinite repetition, the most insidious thing is the gap opened up by repetition – obedient duplication is duplicitous: whence the institute falls. It is that gap, the place within that that hosts the event of the 'outside'. When everything has been thought of, the only thought is 'otherwise'.

DIALOGUES AND DREAMS
IN DIALOGUE WITH SOUMYEN BANDYOPADHYAY:
THE POSITIONING OF YEAR TWO IN BA ARCHITECTURE

EE A 'year two design studio' is the physical and intellectual space which houses the second year design modules; where a student quietly grows from being a year one novice into a student of architecture ready for their third year graduation projects. It can be positioned in different ways; as an autonomous 'year two studio', a 'vertical studio with year three', part of a 'thin' or 'thick sandwich' course or within an 'apprenticeship model' of study. Each comes with its own possibilities.

In 2015, year two 'design studio' at the University of Westminster became autonomous, split from its previous enmeshment as part of a 'vertical studio' with year three. A 'vertical' approach, where students 'practice' in year 2 and then can 'refine and polish' in year 3 can bring about a slicker 'degree show' and impressive refinement of skills. In some ways, a 'horizontal' year structure removes both the safety net of rehearsal and the pressure of performance, with the change in educational context demanding agility, self-belief, judgement and reflexivity. After a more guided first year, the second year became able to act as a more unified and ambitious educational bridge in the journey of the students' development. It supported the steep but natural progression in the complexity of architectural programmes and provided a new space for the synthesis of ideas and their interrogation. The six distinct 'studio groups' which included DS(2)01 linked with the other modules to form a new independent identity for the second year as a whole. The other modules of 'technical studies' and 'cultural context' ran in parallel to, and also appeared formally and informally within the 'design modules'.

If someone had said to me during my own hesitant engagement with my second year of 'formal architecture education' in 1994-95, that twenty years later I would be trusted with leading year two in the BA (Hons) at the University of Westminster, I would have been surprised and curious as to how that had come about. Looking back, I might then have seen a degree in architecture simply as a means to 'becoming an architect' and 'doing architecture', rather than understanding it in relation to 'practicing the possible practices of architecture' and learning how to locate myself in relation to them. If an understanding of architecture education is in the latter category, then BA year two shifts from being perceived as 'the year to get through between starting and finishing' or 'an enormous mountain to climb before the final project', to becoming an 'in-between' opportunity for exploration and experimentation. Not experimentation as seemingly random free-flowing artistic gestures or moves, but carefully enabled by an organised, guided and planned framework within which different architecture practices can be explored and enjoyed. It is with this in mind that DS(2)01 set out its agenda; with no expectation other than to offer the students a sufficiently diverse and personally translatable context; to begin what in some cases becomes a life-long endeavour to find their architectural selves.

SB Since its inception in the late nineteenth century, the Liverpool School of Architecture has always focused its attention on nurturing individual talent in relation to wider intellectual and socio-political concerns. Over the past decades, a distinctive culture of collaborative working has, in addition, developed throughout the School. This is most explicit in the MArch (Part 2), but begins in the second year of our undergraduate (Part 1) course, with aspects of this culture embraced through opportunities gained with the integration of a large cohort of students arriving from our sister university in China, Xi'an Jiaotong-Liverpool University (XJTLU) in Suzhou. The first six weeks of second year are devoted to collaborative working, with the specific aim of putting individual creativity within a wider collaborative culture of cross-fertilisation, realisation and production.

At Liverpool, the second year has always followed a horizontal 'year structure', which has allowed the year to grow its own identity. Unlike the vertical 'unit' system, or different 'units' within a year, the design studios are year-specific, that is, they adhere to a broad agenda for the year, whilst also forming part of extended strands of thematised design investigation running through the School, from second year upwards. These design strands are supported by the research themes of considerable strength within the School, and include: sustainable living and social autonomy; the future ways of living and housing; post-industrial landscape – their curation and reuse; health and wellbeing; the architecture of the institution.

The conversation in the School has always revolved around how robust research and methodological innovation can underpin creative processes. We believe the academic viability of the discipline of architectural design has to rely on a research-centred approach; research by design, to which other forms of research investigation contribute. The second year students are introduced to this culture of investigation, with the broader year theme presented to them as distinctive design themes that respond to both the School's design strands and reflect the positions held by the wide range of full- and part-time teaching staff. The results are certainly diverse but also considered, thought-provoking, and even provocative.

Concerns such as typology, phenomenology and reflective practice underpin the work of the second year, where the initial foundations of these distinctive pedagogic approaches are laid over an already developed understanding of site-specific engagement and an anthropomorphic dimension to design. Underlying all this, however, the second year displays a primary concern for space-making; of spatial manipulation and its testing through model-making. The twin challenges of site and programme – their dialogue articulated through their reading, interpretation, questioning, remaking and mis-reading – provide the creative opportunities for bringing an architectural programme into a spatial reality.

A RIVER RUNS THROUGH IT
DS(2)01: LOST RIVERS AND HIDDEN FRAMEWORKS

When I joined the School of Architecture + Cities as a full-time member of staff in 2015, I led design studio DS(2)01 (first with Anthony Powis and then with Dusan Decermic) as one of the six studios delivering the two major design modules in year two. In DS(2)01, students were encouraged to develop their ability to synthesise new knowledge and to have confidence in their ideas, whilst contextualising their designs in physical places as well as in conceptual spaces. In an endeavour to support students' growth from first to third year, the year two design studio briefs grew in complexity and expectation from semester one to semester two; connected through carefully chosen territories in London, with related, relevant, contemporary themes and building programmes suggested. It was fundamental to the studio's approach that the students' work would be carefully guided and structured, but that the sites offered and briefs issued would allow sufficient flexibility and choice for each student to take ownership, make their own interpretations and develop a personal relationship with their projects.

I have always understood architectural propositions as born from their location, not just physically in terms of material, orientation or programme, but also as part of people's journeys and stories; spaces formed and spatial sequences (inside and outside) for complex woven histories as experienced by past, present and future inhabitants. Architectural propositions are interventions which alter a reality, or realities. This 'alteration' is not something to apologetically minimise, but rather should be seen as something to take great care over; to bravely behold as a new imagined possibility with intentions articulated and impact declared. What does it add, take-away or change; the site, the area, the environment; residents, users and passers by? How can a studio group develop an architecture which is for and serves its people; as individuals and as a collective? In trying to move away from the idea of 'building as object' and towards the creation of spaces for social interaction and reflection, the studio paid particular attention to the way in which institutional buildings sit within the urban fabric, how they affect public and private space, and what physical or symbolic presences they command in the city.

Setting out, or inventing the scenarios for a design studio before the start of each year – 'the design brief' – is the design studio tutor's 'major creative endeavour' and the only part of the year which happens in the absence of the students and their knowledge, ideas and experience. Each year the studio had to be 'launched', or 'offered' to the student cohort, for their consideration and then their selection. DS(2)01 promised to offer (and I quote here from our studio summaries as issued to students at the time): 'a strong contemporary socio-cultural agenda'; 'consideration of architectural inhabitation physically, mentally and spiritually'; 'exploration of how space, light and material quality relates to experience of place'; 'connection to ideas and media from literature, art, philosophy and sociology'; 'an understanding of building typologies in terms of programmatic and symbolic meaning'; 'value given to personal exploratory journeys, building visits and precedent analysis'; 'the emergence through design work of individual student's own cultural values and lived experience'; and a 'sense of shared-purpose and support'. Hopefully the work that follows and the student's own reflections will expose how we fared against our own ambitions and ideals. In September 2015, I did not have a 'three-year plan', but I did know that I wanted to develop coherence in the student's approach and response to the city and building design; one which would set them up with confidence and clarity for future work. I also wanted to develop a framework which naturally allowed for a connection between 'urban' and 'human' through the architecture produced, and which would encourage students to build on thematic possibilities for building programmes which responded to real social, political or economic situations; both locally at the sites of study and more widely beyond.

The lost rivers of London appear and disappear in relation to how the city has changed and grown around them. In addition to offering romantic water-edge sites for projects, the rivers' courses defined clear 'territorial' journeys which led the students from the 'faux-rural' (periphery or green edge), through the 'sub-urban' (predominantly residential or 'domestic') and in to the 'urban' (city or civic 'centre'). Each of the three years began with an ambulant journey following the chosen 'hidden' river. This was positive for studio bonding and for developing skills in map reading, understanding the variety of city scales and urban grains, and learning how to look, how to represent and how to share personal observations and imagine shared futures. These preliminary experiences combined with a study visit half-way through each year (see 'interludes') and were intended to set, develop and maintain a particular understanding and attitude to place. Each year's territorial journeys were paused twice; once for each semester's sites. The processes of investigation, comparison and evaluation carried out by the students to make their choice of site from those offered (or to challenge them completely), led to an enhanced clarity of their criteria or drivers for each project. This, combined with an individual development of the thematic briefs suggested, meant that every student went through the design process with a clear idea of their intentions and a feeling of ownership and authorship of their projects. Mini-projects dotted through the year in parallel to the main design projects, served to simultaneously distract from the pressure of the main project, and focused on a particular approach to design development or an element of the project. These were presented as 'dialogues' for the students to consider; aiming to improve motivation and engagement through honing skills and preventing the dreaded 'design impasse' or 'writer's block'. Instigating deliberate switches in scale and media, from urban to human, or from drawn to modelled to written, helped to nurture an attitude of enquiry and reflection in parallel to ultimately supporting the development of a complete design proposal.

DS(2)01   ELA

HA EVANS + ANTHONY POWIS

15
16

A PUBLIC (IN)CONVENIENCE/DOMESTIC SANCTUARY
SEMESTER 1

A PUBLIC (IN)CONVENIENCE/CIVIC SANCTUARY
SEMESTER 2

FLEETING ENCOUNTERS: PUBLIC (IN)CONVENIENCE

ISHMA AHMED MUSTAFA AKKAYA ARISTIDES APATZIDIS JONES SADIE ALABBASI JASDEEP ATWAL ALEXANDRA BADEA DENISA BALAJ SABINA BLASIOTTI PATRICIA-CYNTHIA BOB IRINA BODROVA NAVPREET BOLINA MIA BRISCOE KATIE BROWN VERONICA CAPPELLI JEFFREY CHAN HANNAH CLARKE GEORGE COSBUC ELLA DALEY STEFAN DEAN ANA DIACONU THUONG DUONG YASEMIN EVMEZ MATTIA FARACI CHRISTINA GELAGOTELLIS KIRIL GEORGIEV DANIEL GLOAMBES ALLASTER GRANT ZUZANNA GRODZKA KATIE HAIGH OLA HJELEN CARLA HORA SABRAH ISLAM ANDREEA ISTRATESCU POLYAN IVANOV MANJOT JABBAL SOOYEON JEONG SHARNA JOHNSON MACIEJ ALEX JUNGERMAN DARINA KEANE SUSANN KERNER YASEMIN KOSE PHILIP LONGMAN BIBIANA MALAWAKULA NABLA MOHAMMAD YAHYA YIANNA MOUSTAKA AHMED MUSTAFA POLINA NOVIKOVA CLARISSA O'DRISCOLL ZUZANNA OSIECKA JAROSLAW OWSIANNY KYU SUNG PAI SIGNE PELNE NICKOLAY PENEV JOSHUA RICKETTS YARA SAMAHA SANDRA SIDAROUS GUY SINCLAIR ZUZANNA SLIWINSKA GADÉ SMITH CATALINA STROE GIA SAN TU SORAIA VIRIATO NABLA MOHAMMAD YAHYA MONIFA YASMIN YAGMUR YURTBULMUS ELINA ZAMPETAKIS TAMAS ZUBERECZ 2015-2016

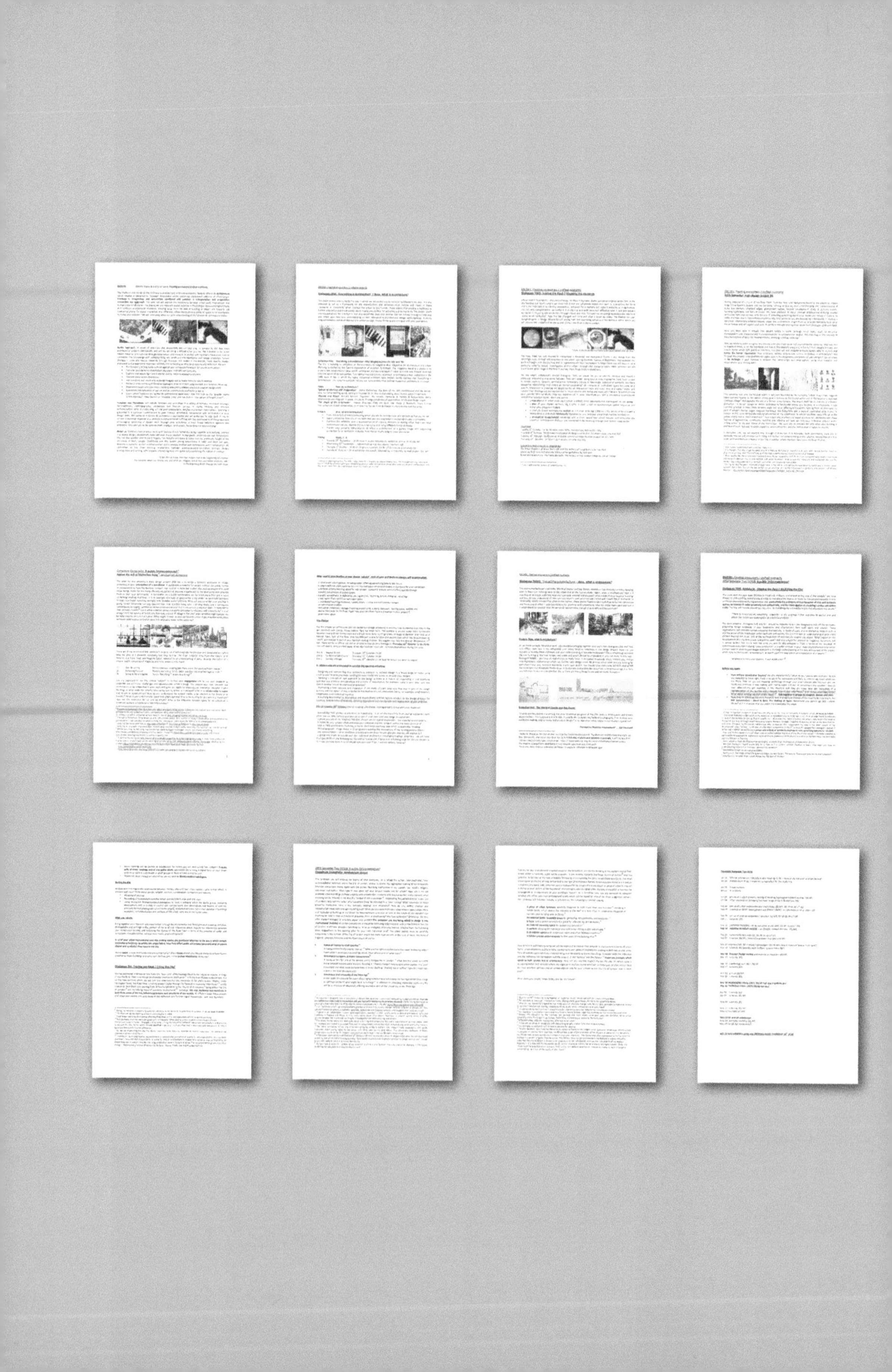

15
16

A PUBLIC (IN)CONVENIENCE/DOMESTIC SANCTUARY
SEMESTER 1

A PUBLIC (IN)CONVENIENCE/CIVIC SANCTUARY
SEMESTER 2

FLEETING ENCOUNTERS: PUBLIC (IN)CONVENIENCE

15
16

SEMESTER 1

SEMESTER 2

15
16

The course of the River Fleet runs from Hampstead Ponds, through Kings Cross, to the Thames at Blackfriars; from 'faux-rural' to 'post-industrial' to 'contemporary-urbane'. This territory enabled an exploration of the physical and symbolic relationships between water, people and architecture, and gave a rich context for the studio's interest in urban scale interventions and human scale inhabitation. The notion of 'sanctuary' was used to develop a brief for a local 'domestic' community proposal in the first semester and a 'civic' scale intervention in the second semester, with a symbolic presence in the City.

A public [in]convenience: Against the cult of frictionless living. Proposal: a 'domestic sanctuary' on one of three given sites near St Pancras Old Church. Once the site of a Roman Crossroads with a shrine dedicated to the 'Lares Compitales' (household deities), this is now an area of rapid gentrification; rituals of sacrifice, offering and domesticity were considered in this proposal for a new launderette with associated community space. Students' own brief development included micro-brewing, pottery-making, coffee-roasting and textile dying; water as precious, and time as sacrificial.

Interlude: studio study visit to Cordoba and Granada. Close attention was paid to the way in which institutional buildings sit within urban fabric, how they effect public / private space and what literal / symbolic presence they have in the city (SEE INTERLUDE I-III, P.67)

A public [in]convenience: Against the status quo. Proposal: a 'civic sanctuary' opposite the Royal Courts of Justice on Fleet Street. A new institutional headquarters was proposed, with projects challenging accepted systems of civic society and considering questions around human rights, education, natural resources, homelessness and freedom of speech.

15
16

A PUBLIC (IN)CONVENIENCE/DOMESTIC SANCTUARY
SEMESTER 1

A PUBLIC (IN)CONVENIENCE/CIVIC SANCTUARY
SEMESTER 2

FLEETING ENCOUNTERS: PUBLIC (IN)CONVENIENCE

<u>*Compitum Compitalia*: **A public [in]convenience?** [5]</u>
<u>**Against the cult of frictionless living** [6]: *sanctuarium domesticus*</u>

The brief for this semester's main design project (DES 2A) is to design a *domestic sanctuary* or refuge, embodied in your **reinvention of a laundrette**. A laundrette is essential for people without the space, money or permanence to have the facilities to wash their clothes at home but is often also used by people with all of those things, either for the more efficient equipment or because a weekly visit to the local laundrette grounds them in their local community.[7] A laundrette, as a public convenience, can be much more than just a room containing washing machines. It is an example of a type of space within a city where its continued presence through functional necessity overlaps with broader social functions. What will you do whilst your washing is going round? What else can you cleanse? Can it be a public living room, a lending library and a community notice-board for digital, written or verbal communications? Can it also provide a physical space in response to local domestic needs?[8] Can it allow a mental space in a world dominated by efficiency and productivity? Is it an escape from the sphere of family and business; a place of refuge in this way? What activities might people not be able/want to carry out at home? What might it mean to local communities, how might it enable encounters between communities and what does this sanctuary mean to the passer-by?

There are three versions of this semester's project, all of which include the provision of a *laundrette* but which take the idea of a *domestic sanctuary* one step further. The three 'subjects' draw from the history of St Pancras, the River Fleet and Regents Canal; respond to an understanding of place, develop the notion of a what a '*public convenience*' might be and have *water* at their heart.

[1]   Well Be[er]ing   Micro-brewery. Making beer from water: the ultimate Public House.[9]
[2]   Pottering Around   Pottery workshop. Earth, water and fire: Industrial heritage to craft.[10]
[3]   Dying to be ecological   Textile Recycling.[11] Water-less dying?[12]

You are expected to use the chosen 'subject' to further your **engagement** and to use your **research** to celebrate the particular challenges and opportunities which it brings. This enables your own interests and enthusiasms to be embedded in your work and gives you space for creativity and innovation. Consider in your thinking: at what **scale** the activity takes place and by whom is it enjoyed? What is its **relationship to water** and its use or conservation? How do you understand the subject matter to be relevant to the future of St Pancras? What is your architectural, social and urban agenda? Who is the building for and why is it important? How will the institution be run and by whom? What is the difference between space for an individual, a collective space or a house for a machine/process?

---

[5] A *public convenience* in the UK historically refers to a public toilet facility; in America this is known as a 'rest room'. Both of these terms are loaded with other connotations. What else could this place be?
Or is there a practical and geographical need for more? http://greatbritishpublictoiletmap.rca.ac.uk/
[6] *The cult of frictionless living* leaves us with little mental space. Our reliance on modern *commodities* and expectation for *convenience* in the everyday purports to make our lives easier and to allow our 'efforts' to be placed elsewhere.
[7] *Long live the laundrette!* See 1) http://goo.gl/HLZ1VH 2) http://goo.gl/MVg5rm 3) http://goo.gl/t9et6j
[8] With the wc and bath long since been incorporated into the modern home, what does this mean for the ritual of bathing?
[9] Whilst pubs may be declining, micro-brewing is getting bigger and bigger, smaller and smaller: expanding http://www.camdentownbrewery.com/the-beers/, makeshift http://www.hammertonbrewery.co.uk/ and minute http://www.lateknightsbrewery.co.uk/the-brewery.html
[10] A community workshop http://www.ceramicsstudio.coop/first-ceramics-class-at-new-cross/ or small scale production line for tiles or bricks? Casting from existing conditions https://en.wikipedia.org/wiki/Rachel_Whiteread. Celebrating the broken https://dicklehman.wordpress.com/2013/04/18/kintsugi-gold-repair-of-ceramic-faults-2/.
[11] http://www.textile-recycling.org.uk/
[12] http://www.greenbiz.com/blog/2014/07/21/waterless-dyeing-processes-clean-clothing-industry

15
16

A PUBLIC (IN)CONVENIENCE/DOMESTIC SANCTUARY
SEMESTER 1

FLEETING ENCOUNTERS: PUBLIC (IN)CONVENIENCE

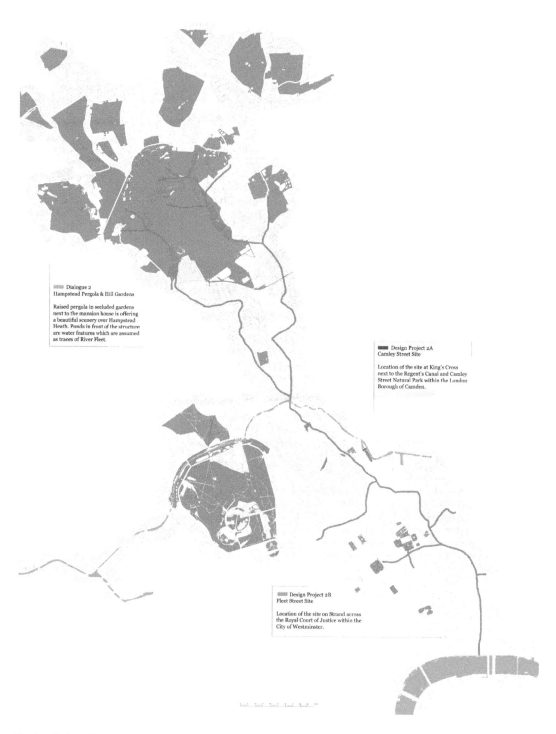

Dialogue 2
Hampstead Pergola & Hill Gardens

Raised pergola in secluded gardens
next to the mansion house is offering
a beautiful scenery over Hampstead
Heath. Ponds in front of the structure
are water features which are assumed
as traces of River Fleet.

Design Project 2A
Camley Street Site

Location of the site at King's Cross
next to the Regent's Canal and Camley
Street Natural Park within the London
Borough of Camden.

Design Project 2B
Fleet Street Site

Location of the site on Strand across
the Royal Court of Justice within the
City of Westminster.

Tracing the fleet, **Yagmur
Yurtbulmus** *(above)*
Zuzanna Osiecka *(opposite)*

TRACING THE FLEET / MAPPING THE MOMENTS

Water can be considered as the font of life. We founded our towns where we could find it and are completely dependent upon it; it quenches our thirst and is the main part in our bodily constitution; we yearn for it mentally but make it work for us in agriculture, industry and transportation; we bathe in it to cleanse and wash away our effluence with it, but also express our belief in its purity and symbolism through rituals and rites. The themes for this year's design projects will spring from the relationship between these understandings of water and the territory within which the subject will be unravelled; the course of the Fleet River in North London. It flows from two sources in Hampstead – Kenwood and Hampstead Ponds – and moves from the seemingly rural, through the suburban to the urban, joining the River Thames at Blackfriars. The journey and experience of the Fleet River was carefully traced by the studio: visible or hidden, static or dynamic, permanent or temporary, natural or man-made, physical or symbolic. Through precision in identification, observation, representation and communication, confidence was built and the use of different media tested by students. The relationships 'between people and water' embodied in the urban journey were explored; in space, built form, or inhabitation. The practical and symbolic moments were brought to light.

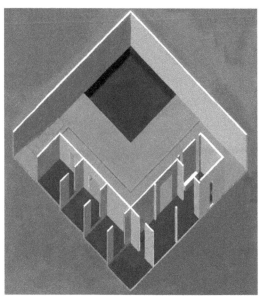

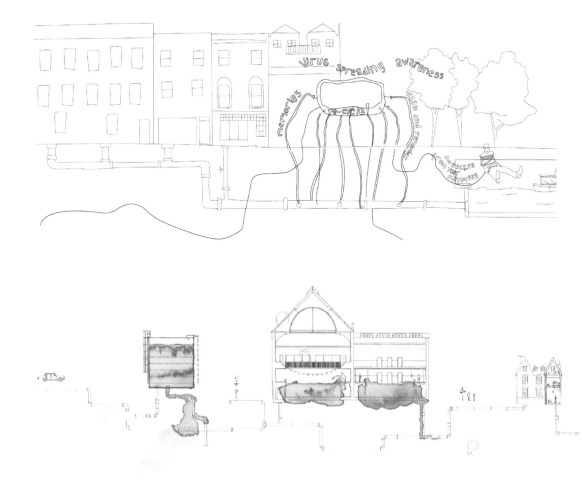

A personal response to brief and programme:
Elina Zampetakis *Domestic refugees (above)* Media: clay,
Hidden people, places and spaces (below, and top p.30)
Kiril Georgiev *Dying to be ecological; textile recycling*
(middle, p.30)

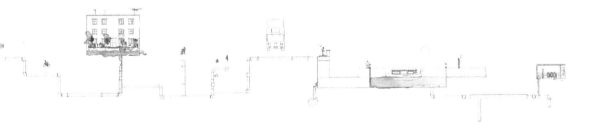

Christina Gelagotellis *A sense of place: impressions from the site at St Pancras Old Church.* Media: oil on canvas.

ALLASTER GRANT
POTTERING AROUND; POTTERY WORKSHOP AND LAUNDRETTE

'A refuge from our tempest' sought to give local residents and visitors the opportunity to escape the hustle and bustle of London life through 'a meditation on pottery'; its crafting and the attention it demands. The proposal consisted of four small buildings, each with a different sensibility coming from their materiality and lighting (see next page). They were composed around a new external space intended to allow semi-private enjoyment of the tree-tops and glimpses of the surroundings.

As the first project in year two, the main aim was to improve an understanding of architecture in terms of materiality and context; through carefully drawn studies of building precedents and by developing a relaxed and exploratory approach to design development. Consideration of space at a human scale and the experience of materials in inhabitation and contextually, were key. Dominant was the presence of Juhani Pallasmaa and Alvar Aalto, with much of the final portfolio dedicated to studies of their buildings and representation techniques. Some time was spent re-drawing the Villa Mairea by Aalto in an attempt to understand the language of the building as an overall composition in relation to its elements and their materiality, colour and texture. The ethos of 'wabi sabi' as finding beauty in the imperfection of natural things added further meaning and clarity to the possibilities of designing in this way.

As an experiment, 'found' materials on site were cast and then re-presented abstractly as a notional street scene; linking touch and texture, memory and imagination.

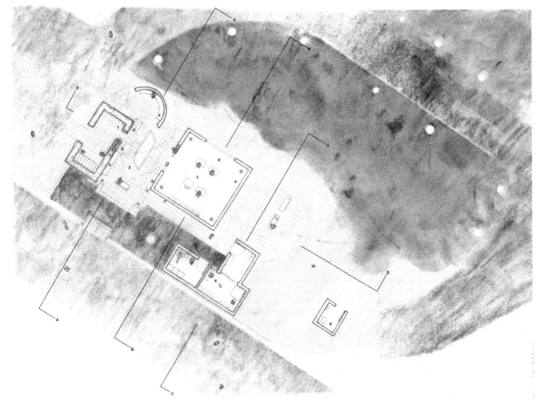

Allaster Grant *Developing a material sensibility; found matter and imagined inhabitations, St Pancras Old Church.* Media: photographs of castings and pencil on paper.

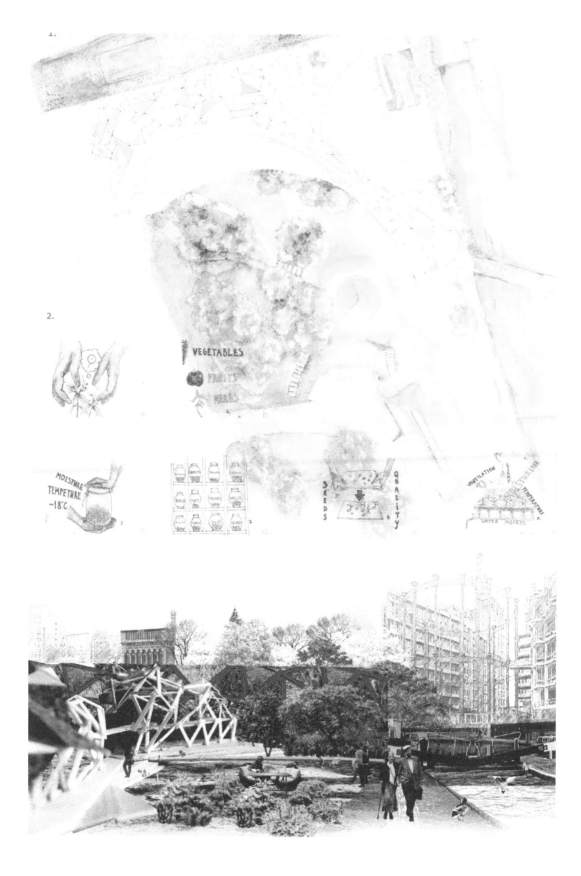

1.

2.

VEGETABLES
FRUITS
HERBS

MOISTURE
TEMPETURE
-18°C

SEEDS

QUALITY

DISTILLATION

WATER ACCESS

IRINA BODROVA
KINGS CROSS SEEDBANK, CAMLEY STREET NATURAL PARK

In response to the site's location and its connection to water, the brief was reinvented to include: a new public garden; spaces for community interaction; and nurturing plants as part of 'relaxation' or 'meditation'. An idea of 'urban farming' developed into designing a new seedbank and greenhouse as part of Camley Street nature reserve. The pedestrian journey through it linked to the new bridge connecting the existing community of St Pancras with the commuter hub at Kings Cross.

Camley Street Natural Park site plan and brief explanation (top, p.38)
Collages of new seed bank, gardens and water tower beyond (bottom, p.38)
Bridging over Regent's Canal to the new seedbank (top, p.39)
An interior; storing seeds and growing tomatoes (bottom, p.39)

GEORGE COSBUC
POTTERING AROUND: LAUNDRETTE, POTTERY WORKSHOP, MEDITATION SPACE

A careful, layered approach to massing aimed to respect the scale of the churchyard and adjacent buildings. Internal and external spaces were designed to fit around the existing mature trees. The site remained a garden to meander and contemplate but with the addition of a shared 'community refuge'. 'Washing time' was passed by making pottery or meditating; cleansing mind and soul. Earlier development was all in charcoal hand-drawings, but this set attempted to imitate that sensibility through digital production.

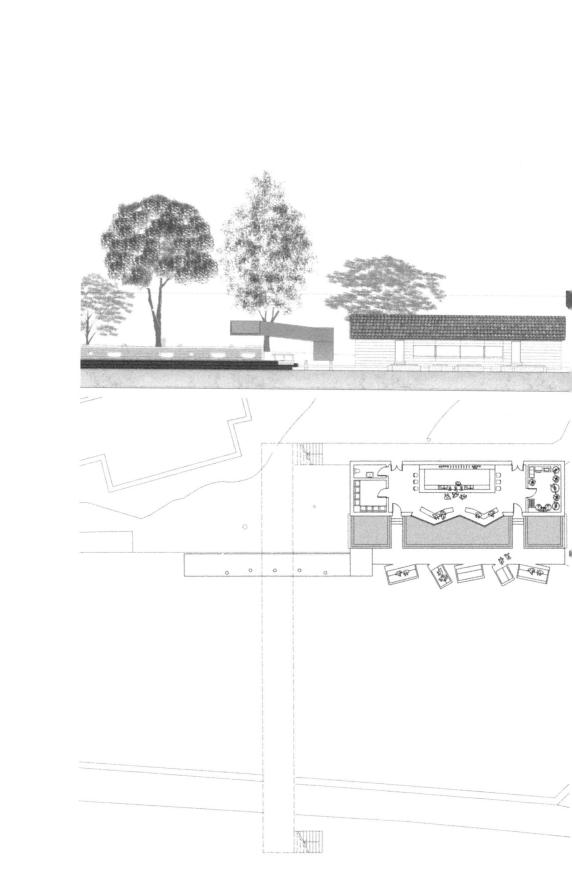

YAGMUR YURTBULMUS
WELL-BEERING; WATER TO BEER

Site and brief were chosen and developed to capitalise on Camden Town's existing micro-brewery and potential future link between the new Kings Cross Coal Drop and Camley Street Natural Park via the new bridge. Located at this pivotal place between the existing community of St Pancras and the commuters of Kings Cross, this project was planned to allow freedom to either just pass it by, or to be willingly captured in the brewery itself; nestled in intimate pods at the water level of Camden Canal. Its understated physical presence respects the existing Camley Lock Cottage and the red brick water tower, taking on their scale and materiality to create a new inhabited edge along the Canal.

2016 Semester Two DES2B: A public [in]convenience?
Compitum Compitalia: sanctuarium civicus

This semester you will develop the theme of *'civic sanctuary'* as a refuge for certain *'non-profitable'/'non-commodifiable'* activities within the City of London, where currently the aggressive trading of contemporary financial institutions shares space with the archaic founding institutions of our society; law, health, religion, education and justice. What type of new space will your project create and for whom? How will it link old accepted understandings of these subjects with modern-day concerns and requirements? In this context, what meaning can be imbued in the idea of a 'festival of the crossroads'[15], celebrating 'household deities' in the City of London? How can the notion of a 'household deity' be manifest in a 'civic' calling? What relevance do these powerful institutions have in our everyday dealings and situations? How do you define physical and metaphorical crossroads through a building brief? What can you learn from your observations about urban fabric and institutional buildings in our cities? Do they represent eras past or look to the future of our society? Can anything be read in their architectural presence, form or positioning? Are they defensive? Offensive? Do they offer shelter? Refuge? Or emanate power and control? **This semester you are being asked to design a new 'institutional' building** which will provide one of the three following organisations with a new home in the City of London. It will also provide a backdrop to, or be an instigator of a new festival. Choose from the following three suggestions as the starting point for your own individual brief. The client bodies must be carefully researched in the context of the City of London and in the more local vicinity of the Inns of Court, the Bank of England, Liberties, Churches and the Royal Courts of Justice.

A　　**National Council for Civil Liberties**[16]

A headquarters for the charity 'Liberty'.[17] What are the rights and freedoms that need defending today? From what is sanctuary required? By whom, from where and on what scale?

B　　**Worshipful Company of Water Conservators**[18]

A headquarters for one of the newest Livery Companies in London.[19] What are the issues currently being debated around water scarcity, flooding or climate change? Where does water appear in a 'civic' household and what social purpose does it serve? Bathing? Sharing tea or coffee? Does fair trade play a part in the brief development?

B　　**Almshouse and University of the Third Age**[20]

A new place of residence for a part of our aging community which relates to the legal profession, clergy or perhaps bankers? Who might need re-homing?[21] In addition to providing residential sanctuary this will be an institute of education, offering courses as part of the University of the Third Age.

---

[15] As explored in Semester One, a Compitalia is a Roman festival of the 'crossroads', celebrating household deities. **How can you define your crossroads in this location and your festival in relation to the brief you develop?** The following text explores the origins and interpretations of this festival in the countryside and in the city. http://dare.uva.nl/document/2/61030

[16] Civil liberties are basic rights and freedoms granted to citizens of a country through national common or statute law. They include freedom of speech, movement, assembly, association and religious worship, and freedom from arbitrary arrest.

[17] 'Liberty' is an independent human rights organisation, founded in 1934, which works to defend and extend rights and freedoms in England and Wales. It is currently led by Shami Chakrabarti. 'Reprieve' is another charity which provides worldwide Legal Aid. Could your building be a headquarters for both lobbying and action?

[18] The Water Conservators are passionate about sustaining and conserving the public requirements of clean water, both for domestic and industrial purposes. They seek to support and promote the advancement of education within the industry.

[19] The livery companies of the City of London comprise London's ancient and modern trade associations and guilds. Liverymen retain voting rights for the senior civic office, such as the Lord Mayor. The Worshipful Company of Water Conservators is one of the 31 'modern' Livery Companies formed in the last 80 years. Almshouses

[20] Almshouses were established from the 10th Century in Britain, to provide a place of residence for poor, old and distressed people by way of charitable housing to enable these people (typically elderly people who can no longer work or earn enough to pay their rent) to live in a particular community.

[21] Do you have a vision for collapse of our systems? Is there a civic function that you predict as obsolete in the future, rendering the educated homeless/profession-less?

15
16

A PUBLIC (IN)CONVENIENCE/CIVIC SANCTUARY
SEMESTER 2

FLEETING ENCOUNTERS: PUBLIC (IN)CONVENIENCE

Allaster Grant *Site plan of Fleet Street showing the location of the project opposite the Royal Courts of Justice.*

ALLASTER GRANT
A HAVEN FOR OUR LIBERTY: HOMELESS HOSTEL AND CAB HQ

Following the first semester inquiry into material and experience of place (p.35) and the study visit to Andalucía (p.67), semester two began with a journey from Kings Cross to Blackfriars. Scale and theme were shifted from 'domestic to 'civic'. Through these explorations, a deeper understanding of urban grain was developed and ways in which a city is woven together were recognised; physically and socially. The project was to design a new HQ for the charity Liberty on a thin site opposite the Royal Courts of Justice on Fleet Street. This proposal used floor texture as a literal and symbolic gesture to the street and within, to represent our democracy; one that sees so many people without a home. Visiting Liberty's existing headquarters, experiencing some public space protests and spending time at venues where missionary or charity work is hosted, helped to inform an architectural and socio-political approach to the design of this new building. It demanded both a strong presence as part of the street-scape and privacy for the inhabitants. A perforated brick exterior skin maintained some (literal and symbolic) transparency and a cobbled street extended from the tight winding streets to the south-west into the ground floor public area opposite the Courts. Internally, vertical connections were made between public and private; views and glimpses give a feeling of support from others and privacy for the individual as needed. A new 'public chapel' was included as part of the building's garden sanctuary, adding to the local sequence of churches and chapels with restricted opening hours, this one would be open any time for peace and contemplation.

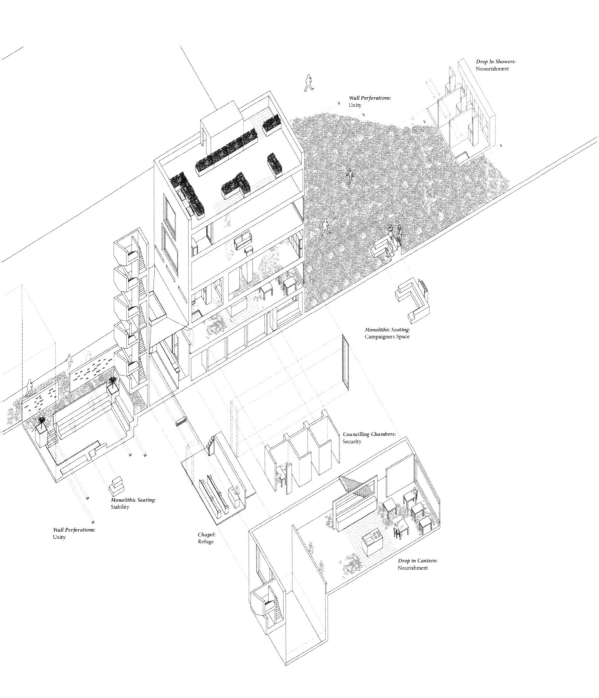

Drop In Showers:
Noourishment

Wall Perforations:
Unity

Monolithic Seating:
Campaigners Space

Councilling Chambers:
Security

Monolithic Seating:
Stability

Wall Perforations:
Unity

Chapel:
Refuge

Drop in Canteen:
Nourishment

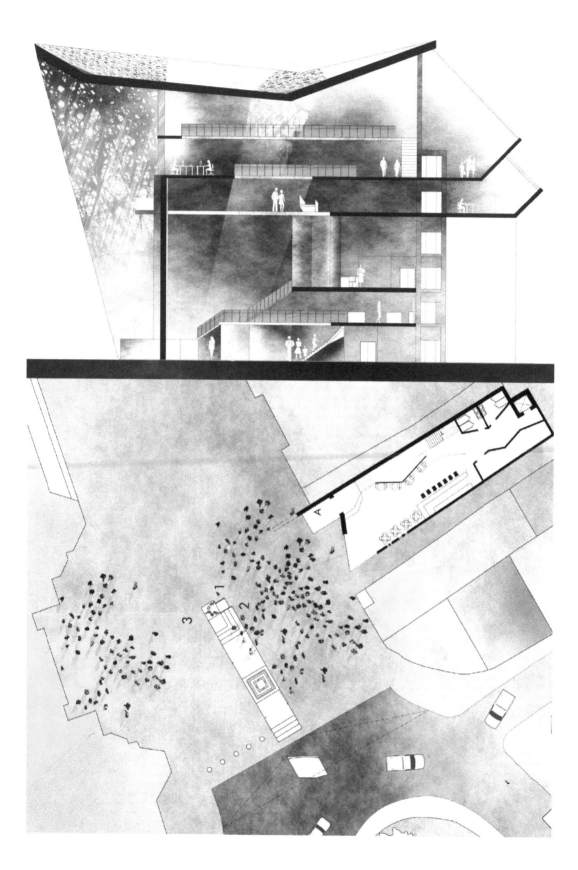

ANA DIACONU
THE PUBLIC MANIFESTO AND SUPPORT CENTRE

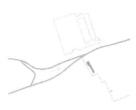

A new National Institute for Civil Liberties placed opposite the Royal Courts of Justice (RCJ). An 'introverted' platform for knowledge and communications is offered through public exhibition spaces and an information centre, with an 'extroverted' platform for 'justice', street occupation and a permanent 'soap box'. Pairing a strong visual presence with a social agenda, the sculptural façade 'challenges' the Courts in mass and formality, with a shimmering roof uplifting speakers below.

Fleet Street elevation (above top)
Internal render of library and exhibition space (above)
Section exploring interior lighting and perforated skin (top, p.50)
Site plan; 'soap box' street demonstration outside RCJ (bottom, p.50)

IRINA BODROVA
THE DEVEREUX WATER CONSERVATORS

The Devereux Water Conservators are responsible for water quality, flooding and climate change. Continuing thematically from semester one's interpretation of the brief to include ecological concerns (see p.39), this project was a response to the ongoing aggressive trading of contemporary financial institutions and lack of shared spaces within the City of London. Law Courts are historically powerful and symbolic in society; oppressive and dictatorial. This scheme brought much needed shared social space for both legal and general discussions to the heart of Fleet Street. Improved accessibility of legal knowledge for the public through a combination of public and private facilities, allowing intermingling in leisure and work. Looking to Scandinavia, bathing was suggested as alternative to the prevalent drinking culture of the City. Through the design development, different media were used to explore communication, representation and the proposed materiality of the new HQ.

Fleet Street elevation (above top)
Model photos exploring skin (above)
Interior render exploring potential
of intermingling leisure and work (opposite)

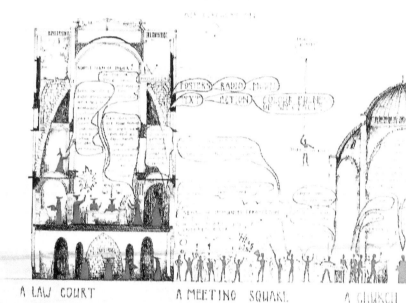

A LAW COURT   A MEETING SQUARE   A CHURCH

ENLIGHTMENT LIBERALISM – DEVELOPMENT OF DEMOCRATIC CULTURE

«THE INTERACTION OF LAW ENDS UP RECREATING THE
CULTURALY AND MORALY»

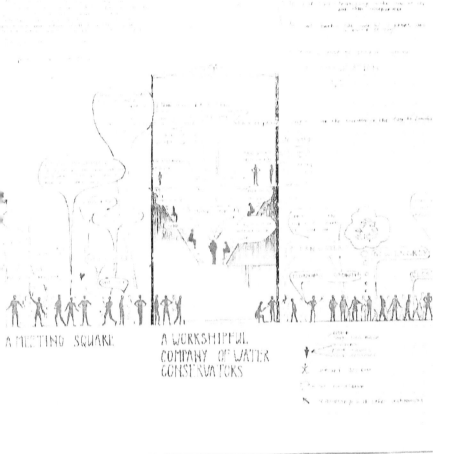

A MEETING SQUARE

A WORKSHIPFUL
COMPANY OF WATER
CONSERVATORS

NOT ONLY MATERIALLY BUT ALSO

Irina Bodrova *Brief and place*
Enlightenment Liberalism – Development of democratic culture

(iv)

(iii)

(ii)

(i)

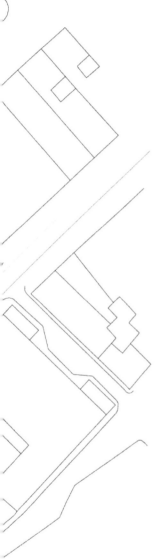

VERONICA CAPELLI

THE UNIVERSITY OF FREE THOUGHT

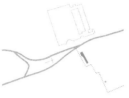

The idea of monastic education is reimagined here within a new university setting. The aim of this project was to create learning spaces for 'free thinking' on 'law, justice and order' opposite the Royal Courts of Justice on Fleet Street. Magisters and caretakers of knowledge (as opposed to law) are brought to and integrated with the public realm. Monastic building typologies were studied and abstracted; first in the brief development and then in the architectural proposition. The cellular, the communal and the journey between were expressed and reconfigured. The different stages of learning and the need for openness and peace through all, from 'ignorance' (darkness) to 'revelation' (light), were explored in the material and spatial qualities of each level.

The building is open to the street (i), with a forest of columns at the upper-ground level encouraging exploration between and offering privacy within. The columns penetrate all levels (iv) and sound travels through them like organ pipes; a gentle buzz or whistle of brains working noticeable throughout. There are darker, individual spaces inside the columns at a lower level for private study and light-filled open spaces at the higher levels (ii+iii) for knowledge exchange and inspiration.

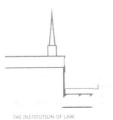

THE INSTITUTION OF LAW

THE INSTITUTION OF KNOWLEDGE

GUY ADAMS SCOTT BATTY
STEFANIA BOCCALETTI
STEPHEN BROOKHOUSE SAM
CADY FABIO CARDOSO DE
LEMOS CARVALHO DUSAN
DECERMIC JENNY DUNN
ELANTHA EVANS GEORGIA
FOLLETT AARON FOX JOHN
GRIFFITHS CLARE HAMMAN
DAVID HAWKINS KATE JORDAN
CONSTANCE LAU HWEI FAN
LIANG JAMILEH MANOOCHEHRI
ALISON MCLELLAN SARAH
MILNE NEGIN GHORBANI
MOGHADDAM NATALIE
NEWEY JOHN NG ANDREW
PECKHAM EMMA PERKIN
ANTHONY POWIS CLAIRE
PRIEST SHAHED SALEEM ANA
SERRANO JEANNE SILLETT
JACOB SZIKORA TSZWAI SO
MATTHEW STEWART OCTAVIA
STAN EMMA THOMAS
VICTORIA WATSON CAMILLA
WILKINSON SHUYING XU
FIONA ZISCH   2015-2016

When we named the 2016-17 studio 'urban ghosts', (see p.93) it was an attempt to encourage thinking about the city as something continually made and re-made, built and re-built over an extant archaeology of elements and processes. Architecture in this context is always 'repair-work', a term opposed to 'construction', which implies an a-temporal moment of creation. Students had to deal with compromises with past uses, to consider current traces and imagine possible futures. These aren't separate processes: the ghosts, of course, are not the relics themselves, but the ways in which we see them, recombining them with our own understandings of what they might have been, and what they might be next. The previous year had seen students grapple with a churchyard that had been substantially reorganised once already (by Thomas Hardy, to make way for a railway) and then to reconsider a building then under reconstruction, fully contained within scaffold and debris netting; as a conceit to allow freedom of thought.

The move from working closely with the historic, now mostly subterranean River Fleet (2015-16), to siting projects along the New River (a 45km artificial waterway) shifted the organising device from a 'lost' river to 'remnant' pieces of industrial infrastructure. The New River cuts through and dictates the layout of the terraces known as Harringay Ladders, prompting questions about the ways in which different urban layers subtend others, and how negotiations between elements of the city might resolve spatially. Projects sited around the edge of a reservoir made bold interventions, whilst others took a picturesque approach to framing the water-landscape. Later projects for Mitre Square near Aldgate were haunted by the ghosts of past occupancies and preoccupied with contemporary social problems. This work of layering, drawn from close attention to the built and spontaneous (persistent and fleeting) strata of London, is a practice learnt from close attention to sites as ghosts.

TUTOR REFLECTION
ANTHONY POWIS: DS(2)01 DESIGN STUDIO TUTOR 2015-2017

ISHMA AHMED MUSTAFA AKKAYA ARISTIDES APATZIDIS JONES
SADIE ALABBASI JASDEEP ATWAL ALEXANDRA BADEA DENISA
BALAJ SABINA BLASIOTTI PATRICIA-CYNTHIA BOB IRINA BODROVA
NAVPREET BOLINA MIA BRISCOE KATIE BROWN VERONICA
CAPPELLI JEFFREY CHAN HANNAH CLARKE GEORGE COSBUC ELLA
DALEY STEFAN DEAN ANA DIACONU THUONG DUONG YASEMIN
EVMEZ MATTIA FARACI CHRISTINA GELAGOTELLIS KIRIL GEORGIEV
DANIEL GLOAMBES ALLASTER GRANT ZUZANNA GRODZKA KATIE
HAIGH OLA HJELEN CARLA HORA SABRAH ISLAM ANDREEA
ISTRATESCU POLYAN IVANOV MANJOT JABBAL SOOYEON JEONG
SHARNA JOHNSON MACIEJ ALEX JUNGERMAN DARINA KEANE
SUSANN KERNER YASEMIN KOSE PHILIP LONGMAN BIBIANA
MALAWAKULA NABLA MOHAMMAD FATEMAH MOHAMMADI
YAHYA YIANNA MOUSTAKA AHMED MUSTAFA POLINA NOVIKOVA
CLARISSA O'DRISCOLL ZUZANNA OSIECKA JAROSLAW OWSIANNY
KYU SUNG PAI SIGNE PELNE NICKOLAY PENEV JOSHUA RICKETTS
YARA SAMAHA SANDRA SIDAROUS GUY SINCLAIR ZUZANNA
SLIWINSKA GADÉ SMITH CATALINA STROE GIA SAN TU SORAIA
VIRIATO NABLA MOHAMMAD YAHYA MONIFA YASMIN YAGMUR
YURTBULMUS ELINA ZAMPETAKIS TAMAS ZUBERECZ

00:55:38 I mean, I don't know about everyone else but for me at the time I was always reticent to show something that I felt was not of a certain standard, when in reality there is value in the scrappiness to convey the beginnings of an idea.

00:55:57 Is that in practice or at university?

00:56:03 In both really. I go back to crits as a visiting critic and the work that tutors are more interested in now are not polished which is the exact opposite of what I would have done when I was a student.

00:56:10 So they prefer the work in progress.

00:56:15 Of course, you can visualise the thought process behind it. I just wonder if I did not explore enough in second year because I tried to get everything perfect for crits.

00:56:30 And that's come about through your reflection of the book, has it not?

00:56:34 Does anyone else feel like they should have explored more in their undergraduate degree or second year?

00:56:43 I think the pressure we were talking about earlier was self-inflicted, like I put pressure on myself, which can be very debilitating to the design process.

00:57:08 I had such a naïve approach to architecture, I was so focused on the theory, I spent most of my time in the library reading rather than working in studio. I was not comparing my work to others as my workspace was on the other side of the building, so any pressure and self-doubt I experienced was all internalised.

00:58:02 Seeing everyone else's projects presented this way in the book, however, has been great. I think we

STUDENT REFLECTIONS
DS2(01) REFLECTING BACK ON SECOND YEAR AND BA DEGREE
CONVERSATION TOOK PLACE ON ZOOM 19 JULY 2020

were always too stressed during crits to fully appreciate the studio's work.

00:58:40 Or not sleeping the night before! Saying that, I have realised with my Master's I have not had an all-nighter at all, whereas in Westminster I only had all-nighters. I don't know where the difference is coming from.

and actually focusing on the brief. First year gave me the foundational skills – I had a primary grasp of the softwares available. Second year was more than just a transitional period; I learnt how to develop a dialogue with the brief as we've said, and how to think more critically about my architecture, it's relationship to the

LOOKING AT ALL THOSE BEAUTIFUL SKETCHES – THOSE WERE ACTUALLY THE ONES THAT I WAS LEAST PROUD OF AND I KEPT THEM HIDDEN... WHEN IN REALITY THEY ARE THE ONES THAT EVOKE THE MOST

00:59:52 Is there an appreciation of your own time that comes from working in practice perhaps?

01:00:03 Yes and I also think, like you were saying, we put so much pressure on ourselves to create this great design and present it as perfectly as possible. However, we end up being too tired to articulate the concept and programme of the design proposal and in doing so forget how to even express what we want to present. So, I think it is the pressure that affects our judgement which is imposed by us more than the tutors.

01:00:41 I agree. When I was doing the undergraduate degree I was so determined on having that beautiful final drawing for every crit that I forgot about the process of learning

site and to the users. All of this made final year easier.

I did not realise it at the time though. Like everyone, I prioritised the final drawings for portfolio and forgot about the development process and how important it was to my education. Now looking at the book and looking at all those beautiful sketches – those were actually the ones that I was the least proud of and I kept them hidden during presentations. When in reality they are the ones that evoke the most.

01:02:00 Ideas that are jotted down on paper tend to be the best and the ones you come back to time and time again.

ILLUSTRATIONS

The study visits in 2015-16 and in 2017-18 took DS(2)01 to Andalucía in Spain. Cordoba and Granada were chosen not only for their thrilling history, natural beauty and architectural prowess, but more precisely to introduce the themes and scale of study for the second semester design projects. The visits took place right at the start of semester to reinvigorate the students after the break and an agenda for new ways of looking and understanding space and place. Ideas explored during semester one were also reinforced; particularly the architectural manifestation of notions of domestic or civic, an interest in water practically and symbolically, and the interrogation of a building's active role within a city. The trips revolved around four key visits: to the Mezquita in Cordoba and its surrounding labyrinthine streets, and to the Alhambra in Granada sitting across from the multitude of houses in the Albaycin facing it.

These pairings took an understanding of built urban context beyond the visual, and of the manifestation of architecture beyond the object. Exploring what impact power, politics and resources have on the development of a city was key in setting up a response to briefs given in semester two. Observations and interests were compared thematically between Spain and London by the students through their study drawings, impressions and photography; exploring scale, culture and power, and consideration of the place of the 'institution' within city and society. Before returning to London and the second semester projects, the role of the 'plaza' in both spatial urban sequences and as the core of local social life was observed and mapped. Remembering that 'there is no outside' just 'in-betweens', particular attention was given to threshold spaces between 'inside' and 'outside' as they mediate between city, building and person.

15 17
16 18

CHASING THE PAST / EXCITING THE CITY

INTERLUDE I,III: RHYTHM ANALYSIS POWER PEOPLE

i, ii

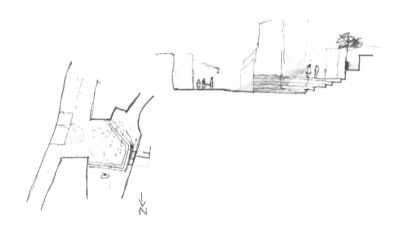

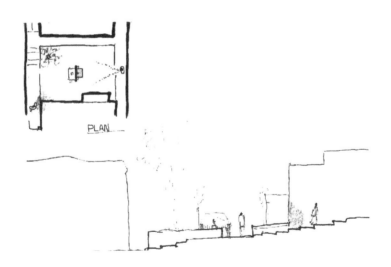

PLAN

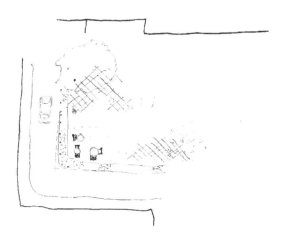

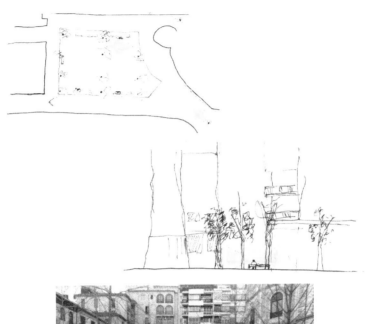

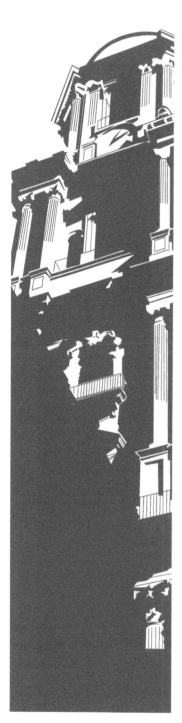
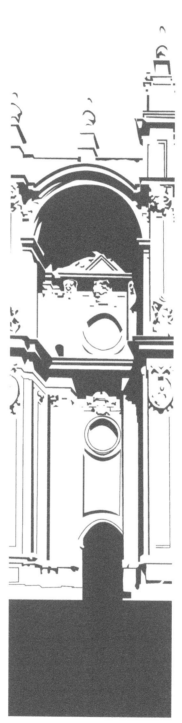

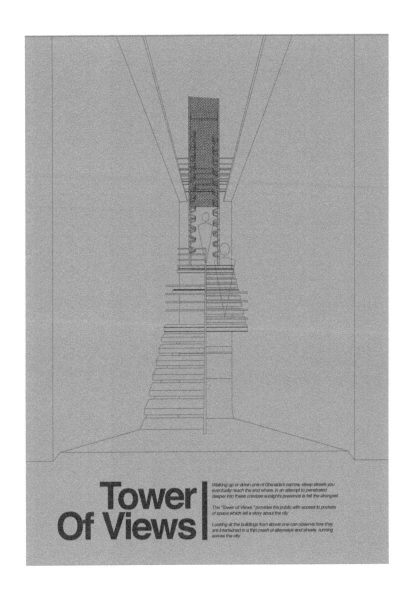

Tower Of Views

Walking up or down one of Granada's narrow, steep streets you eventually reach the end where, in an attempt to penetrated deeper into these crevices sunlight's presence is felt the strongest.

The "Tower of Views " provides the public with access to pockets of space which tell a story about the city

Looking at the buildings from above one can observe how they are intertwined in a thin mesh of alleyways and streets running across the city

Because of the dence arrangement of housing blocks in the city center the emount of natural light inside the building is limited. The integration of open tall courtyards helps solve the problem. A space neither outside nor in its charecter is constantly changing.

Prior to entering the Alhambra we entered the p
area surrounding the complex through a gate w
made the transition from the fabric of the city t
fabric of nature.

Sunlight was illuminating the tree crowns penet
through the golden colour of the leaves.

Two streams of water are running on both sides
the pathway. Each molecule encounters numerc
coble stones in it's path towards the city.

It sounds peaceful, a meditative atmosphere in
way.

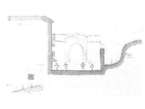

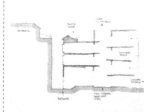

Walking up or down one of Grenada's narrow, steep streets you eventually reach the end where, in an attempt to penetrated deeper into these crevices sunlight's presence is felt the strongest.

Prior to entering the Alhambra we entered the park area surounding the complex through a gate which nade the transition from the fabric of the city to the fabric of nature. What follows is (Section 4)

The M3A is Cordoba's modern art gallery and the observation pf a threshhold condition I made at the entrance of the main gallery space where one needs to go through an opening into a wide wall with two sets of high narow rotating doors. Compared to normal openings where one does not consider the space of transition as a space bu definitione herethe space is infused with importance. It gives the viewer a glimps of what is inside, It once in it, the lack of light and the dark colour of every surface feel like you are about to witness the beginning of a theatrical play just as the curtains are about to open. And then you are there. Into the space. A 4 Stroy height space

THE STAGE IS SET.

The Nacional Palace of Culture in Cordoba presents the visitors with an interesting way of entering a building. One first enters the plaza noticeing the paterned lines in red stone underneath it's feet. As you go up the stairs you reach different landings which give you the chance to look back and examine your achievment. As you reach the top you enevitably look back and see the 58 stairs you had to climb and for the first time can observe the Islamic pattern as a whole standing high up in the position of a viewer. Yhe plza az the object of interest.

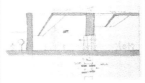

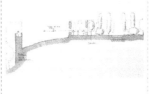

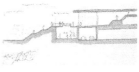

posite the Funky Cordoba hostel is an Interesting ndition of transition from the street space through gate into a modern simple and clean courtyard o's purpose to provide light to the inside spaces of e building frames the sky and isoletes one from the on of the sity as they know it. A second courtyrd ther away provides view through the whole length the building on ground level.

A long curved path leades all tourists to the main area of the Alhambra complex. A simple exercise of framing a view of the city, the vegetation on both sides extend high in the air and one can only look through the small oppenings on each side. As if nature expresses the importance of what is to follow and tries to arrange the surrounding to the background.

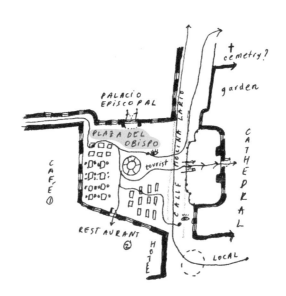

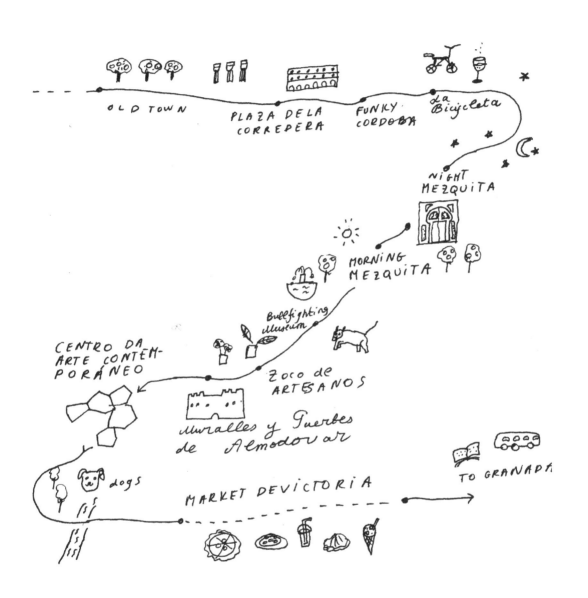

OLD TOWN

PLAZA DE LA CORREDERA

FUNKY CORDOBA

La Bicicleta

NIGHT MEZQUITA

MORNING MEZQUITA

Bullfighting Museum

CENTRO DA ARTE CONTEM-PORÁNEO

Zoco de ARTESANOS

Murralles y Puertes de Almodovar

dogs

MARKET DE VICTORIA

TO GRANADA

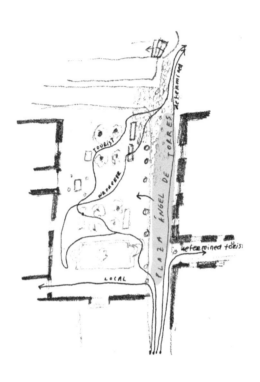

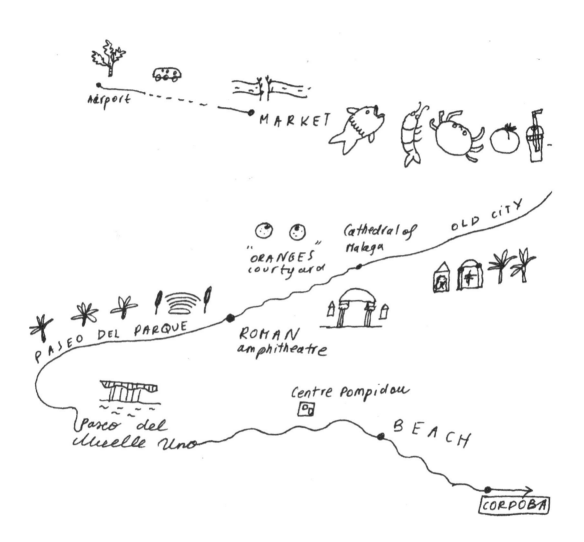

Airport

MARKET

"ORANGES" courtyard

Cathedral of Malaga

OLD CITY

PASEO DEL PARQUE

ROMAN amphitheatre

Paseo del Muelle Uno

Centre Pompidou

BEACH

CORDOBA

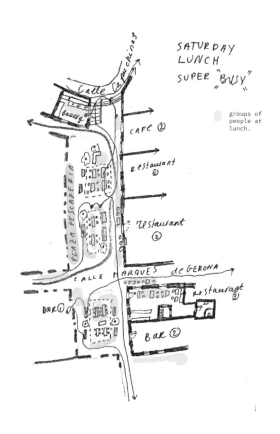

SATURDAY
LUNCH
SUPER "BUSY"

groups of
people at
lunch.

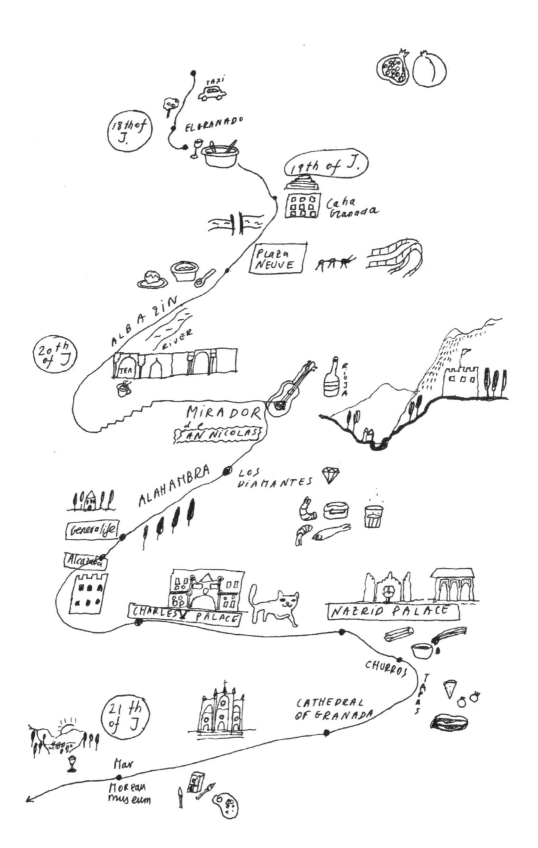

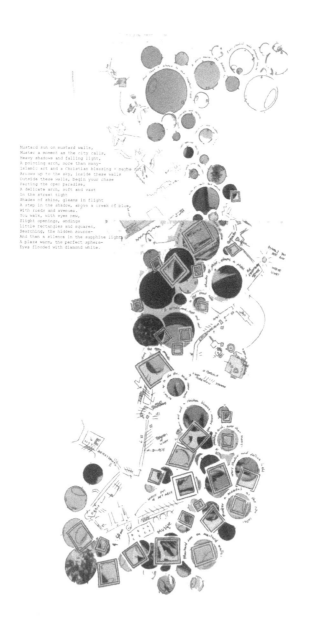

Mustard sun on mustard walls,
Muster a moment as the city calls,
Heavy shadows and falling light,
A pointing arch, more than many-
Islamic art and a Christian blessing - maybe not,
Arrows up to the sky, inside these walls
Outside these walls, begin your chase
Parting the open paradise,
A delicate arch, soft and vast
In the street tight
Shades of shine, gleams in flight
A step in the shadow, above a creek of blue,
With roads and avenues.
You walk, with eyes new,
Slight openings, endings
Little rectangles and squares,
Searching, the hidden source-
And then a silence in the sapphire light,
A plaza warm, the perfect sphere-
Eyes flooded with diamond white.

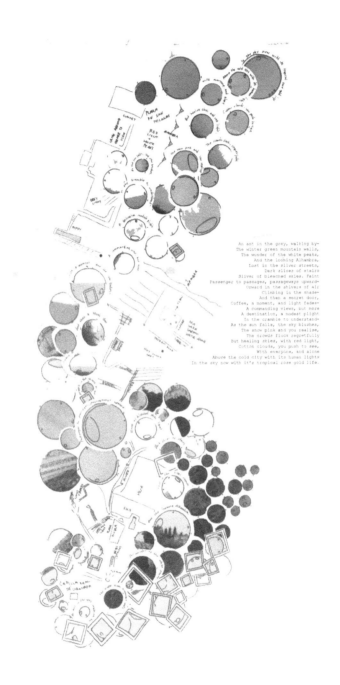

An ant in the grey, walking by~
The winter green mountain walls,
The wonder of the white peaks,
And the looming Alhambra,
Lost in the silver streets,
Dark slices of stairs
Sliver of bleached skies. Faint
Passenger to passages, passageways upward~
Onward in the shivers of air
Climbing in the shade~
And then a secret door,
Coffee, a moment, and light fades~
A commanding views, but more
A destination, a modest plight
In the cramble to understand~
As the sun falls, the sky blushes,
The snow pink and you realise,
The crowds flock regretfully
But healing skies, with red light,
Cotton clouds, you push to see,
With everyone, and alone
Above the cold city with its human lights
In the sky now with it's tropical rose gold life.

DS(2)01   ELA

IA EVANS + ANTHONY POWIS

16
17

THE NEW RIVER:

REDUNDANT / (RE)IMAGINED / SOCIAL HUB
SEMESTER 1

REDUNDANT / REIMAGINED / CIVIC COG
SEMESTER 2

REDUNDANT / [RE]IMAGINED

ISHMA AHMED MUSTAFA AKKAYA ARISTIDES APATZIDIS JONES SADIE ALABBASI JASDEEP ATWAL ALEXANDRA BADEA DENISA BALAJ SABINA BLASIOTTI PATRICIA-CYNTHIA BOB IRINA BODROVA NAVPREET BOLINA MIA BRISCOE KATIE BROWN VERONICA CAPPELLI JEFFREY CHAN HANNAH CLARKE GEORGE COSBUC ELLA DALEY STEFAN DEAN ANA DIACONU THUONG DUONG YASEMIN EVMEZ MATTIA FARACI CHRISTINA GELAGOTELLIS KIRIL GEORGIEV DANIEL GLOAMBES ALLASTER GRANT ZUZANNA GRODZKA KATIE HAIGH OLA HJELEN CARLA HORA SABRAH ISLAM ANDREEA ISTRATESCU POLYAN IVANOV MANJOT JABBAL SOOYEON JEONG SHARNA JOHNSON MACIEJ ALEX JUNGERMAN DARINA KEANE SUSANN KERNER YASEMIN KOSE PHILIP LONGMAN BIBIANA MALAWAKULA NABLA MOHAMMAD YAHYA YIANNA MOUSTAKA AHMED MUSTAFA POLINA NOVIKOVA CLARISSA O'DRISCOLL ZUZANNA OSIECKA JAROSLAW OWSIANNY KYU SUNG PAI SIGNE PELNE NICKOLAY PENEV JOSHUA RICKETTS YARA SAMAHA SANDRA SIDAROUS GUY SINCLAIR ZUZANNA SLIWINSKA GADÉ SMITH CATALINA STROE GIA SAN TU SORAIA VIRIATO NABLA MOHAMMAD YAHYA MONIFA YASMIN YAGMUR YURTBULMUS ELINA ZAMPETAKIS TAMAS ZUBERECZ 2016-2017

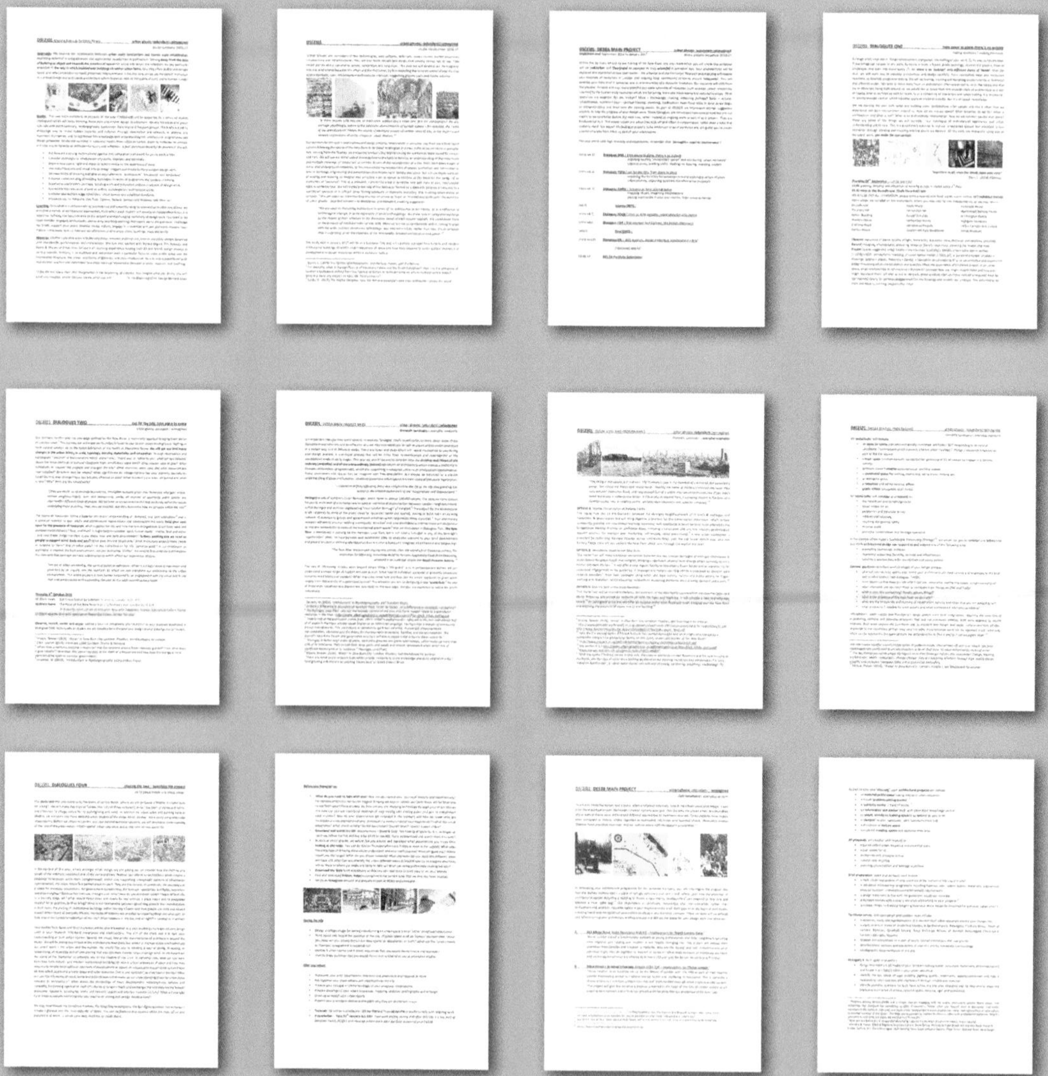

16
17

THE NEW RIVER:

REDUNDANT / (RE)IMAGINED / SOCIAL HUB
SEMESTER 1

REDUNDANT / REIMAGINED / CIVIC COG
SEMESTER 2

REDUNDANT / [RE]IMAGINED

SEMESTER 1

16
17

SEMESTER 2

16
17

The 'New River' was constructed to bring fresh water into central London from Hertfordshire, through the hills of North London, to its 'head' in Islington. This territory offered diverse contexts and enabled an exploration of the multiple meanings of 'resources' as intrinsic drivers of the development of a city. 'Urban Ghosts' are reminders of lost technologies, past cultures, defences, supply routes, buried structures, inhabitations and infrastructures; but they are also those people and places that society chooses not to see.

Urban ghosts redundant/(re)imagined. Proposal: a new 'Social Hub' on one of a choice of three sites linking with local health services to provide new facilities for social prescribing, conduct disorder or hydrotherapy. The sites clustered around this expansive but overlooked part of the New River as it progresses through Harringey and Hackney, bisecting streets and defining odd and unexpected urban pockets.

Notions of sanctuary, domesticity and human interactions were considered key as part of knitting the proposals into a modified urban journey.

Interlude: studio study visit to Madrid, Chinchón, Ávila, and Toledo paid particular close attention to 'urban ghosts' and how they appear today, suggestive of past cultures, lost technologies and their architectural manifestations. (SEE 'INTERLUDE II', P.149)

Urban ghosts redundant/(re)imagined. Proposal: a new 'Civic Cog' on a choice of two liminal sites, shifting from the course of the New River to incorporate a relationship with the City of London. Perceived as a civic sanctuary or everyday asylum; incorporating a public space, charity HQ and small-scale support services. Students interrogated what an 'asylum' could be as a place of refuge, sanctuary and care, nurturing knowledge, communications and understanding.

REDUNDANT / (RE)IMAGINED / SOCIAL HUB
SEMESTER 1

REDUNDANT / REIMAGINED / CIVIC COG
SEMESTER 2

THE NEW RIVER: REDUNDANT / [RE]IMAGINED

"The thing in the square is a reservoir. The truncated cone is the remnant of a windmill that powered a pump. The curves are traces of a round pond... Passing the home of Dickens's mistress the route then runs beneath Petherton Road, ordinary enough but of a width that would be inexplicable if you didn't know there was a watercourse below. It fills a lake in Clissold Park. A pumping station in the form of a Scottish castle, now a climbing centre, watches twin reservoirs now used for canoeing." [8]

OPTION A: Mental Conservation at Railway Fields.

This 'social hub' lies on the boundary between the Haringey *Neighbourhoods* of *St Ann's & Harringay* and *Tottenham & Seven Sisters* and will bring together provisions for the Conservation Volunteers [which include community growing and educational learning resources] with additional support services to be offered by the Bridgehouse Medical Practice on Umfreville Road; including a co-located CAB and low intensity psychological support services [for example peer mentoring, befriending, social prescribing]. [9] A new urban connection is proposed by continuing Haringey Passage across Umfreville Road, past the old 'sewer stench pipe' and into Railway Fields. How will you address the New River which runs through the west of the site?

OPTION B: Woodberry Down to the New River.

This 'social hub' will make a physical connection between the two London Boroughs of Haringey [*Tottenham & Seven Sisters Neighbourhood*] and Islington, bridging a significant physical level change which currently forms a barrier between the two. [10] It will offer a new regular facility to Woodberry Down School and an opportunity for occasional engagement to the passer-by. A language and historic learning centre is proposed for children with conduct disorders [11] from both boroughs using water and local history, nature and public service to trigger learning and relaxation, whilst educating residents on increasing problems around water demand and supply. [12]

OPTION C: And the Rest at the West Reservoir.

This 'social hub' will be located in Hackney, but connects to the NHS Health Centre which includes the Cedar and Heron Practices, patronised by residents of both Haringey and Hackney. It will provide a new hydrotherapy centre [13] on Springpark Drive and will offer an outpost in the West Reservoir itself, bridging over the New River and enjoying the potential of views, sun [!] and bathing. [14]

---

[8] Moore, Rowan [2016], 'Water' in *Slow Burn City* [London: Picador], see blackboard for excerpt.
[9] http://www.centreforwelfarereform.org/uploads/attachment/339/social-prescribing-for-mental-health.pdf
http://www.lowcommission.org.uk/dyn/1435582011755/ASA-report_Web.pdf
[10] How are the demographics different in these two London boroughs and what might be achieved by a connection using a new educational facility on this quiet, underused section of the New River?
[11] http://www.rcpsych.ac.uk/pdf/JCP-MH%20primary%20care%20(March%202012).pdf
[12] See section 4.2.3 http://www.urban-graphics.co.uk/pdf/Haringey-Local-Plan-2013_FINAL-online.pdf
[13] https://www.ncbi.nlm.nih.gov/pmc/articles/PMC3249697/
[14] With the Castle Climbing Centre to one side, Woodberry Wetlands on East Reservoir and the new housing to the North, can the idea of restorative bathing be added to the existing recreation and conservation? A 'Lido', 'Victorian Bathhouses', or other water-based rehabilitation/training, swimming, breathing, meditating? *"To*

16
17

REDUNDANT / [RE]IMAGINED / SOCIAL HUB
SEMESTER 1

THE NEW RIVER: REDUNDANT / [RE]IMAGINED

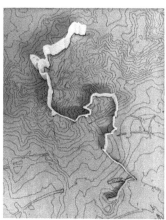

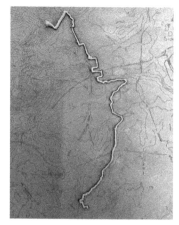

Stefan Dean and Josh Ricketts
Running for the hills? (opposite);
Gadé Smith *Site exploration:*
The New River Walk and
Primrose Hill (above);
Philip Longman *Topographical*
studies (left)

THE NEW RIVER/
OUTWARD BOUND:
RUNNING FOR THE HILLS

Our territory for 2016-17 had one edge defined by the New River and the other by the Roman Road into London. The New River is a man-made aqueduct which once brought fresh water to London-town; the Roman road was an important piece of infrastructure in defence and arrival for connectivity and isolation. The theme of 'resources' and (self) 'defence' formed the basis for this year's understanding of 'domestic' and 'civic institutions' and was a key consideration in the urban and architectural explorations and observations which started the year. Walking from the river's head at Roseberry Avenue to Alexandra Palace enabled experience of many changes in the urban fabric; in scale, typology, density, materiality and occupation. Encouragement was also given to try to expose elements of place that are read subconsciously but still affect our experience of space. Beyond city scale resources, consideration and observation of what 'resources' and 'defences' people 'need' to support their mind, body and soul. What goes beyond physicality and what institutions embody these needs and at what scales; for the individual or in relation to notions of 'common good'?

Leisure along
the New River

New River Path

New River Path

Railway Fields
Nature Park

The New River
Today

Finsbury Park

Finsbury Park
Athletics

Reservoir

Hornsey Water
Treatment Works
and Filter Beds

Functioning
Utilities along
the New River

Sluce House

2000

Water
Works

Electricity
Substation

1950

Former Pumping Station
Now an Art Gallery

1900

The New River
Late 1800s

Functioning
Utilities along
the New River

Reservoir

Filtration
Beds

Stench
Pipe

Hornsey
Pumping
Station

Pump
House

Key:-

New River

Visible body of water

Subterranean water channel

Subterranean body of water
(Reservoirs and Filter Beds)

Former body of water

Operational infrastructure
building

Underground structure

Decommissioned/Re-purposed
building

Demolished structure

Use unkown

Public leisure space

Privately owned public path

Private leisure space

Scale
1:10000

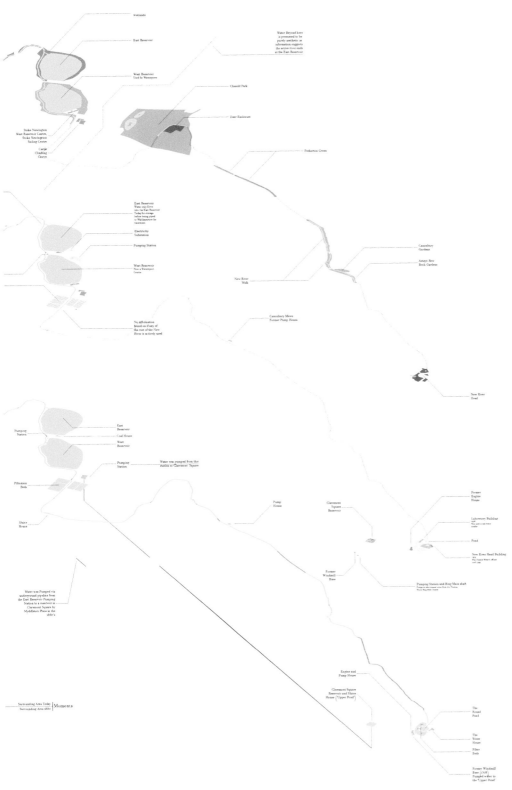

Josh Ricketts *Infrastructure along The New River 1880-2016*

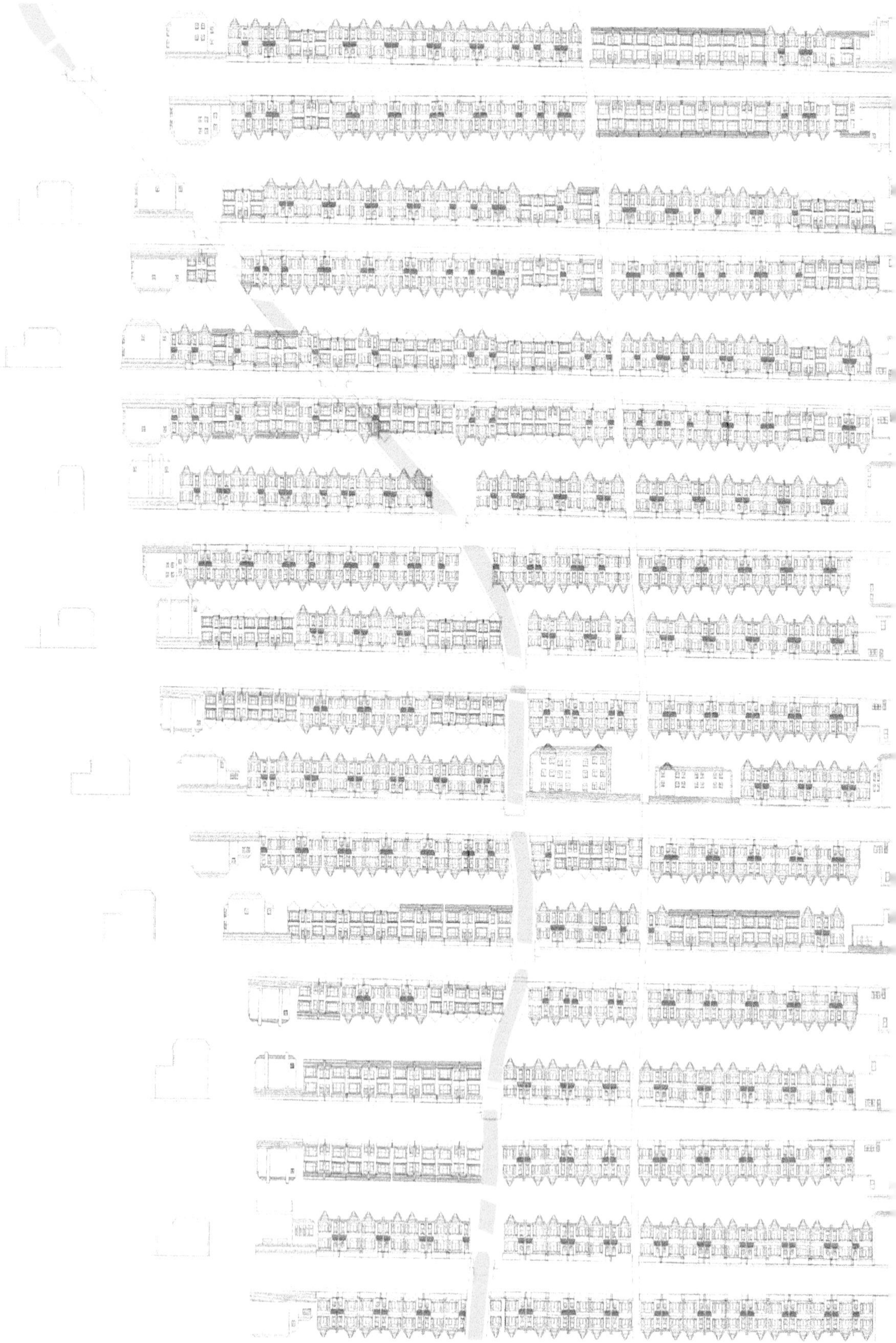

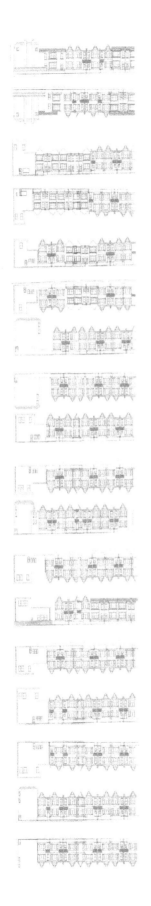

This project proposed a new co-located Citizens Advice Bureau integrated with local NHS practices; with additional provision for a low intensity psychological services centre; thematically focussed on developing spaces for meditation and art therapy. The project aimed to improve urban connectivity through Railway Fields with individual spaces for meditation carefully placed as part of the existing landscape. Anonymous urban grain and individual personal pain were explored through a series of models and drawings.

Stefan Dean *First iteration of models exploring enclosed space for meditation and art therapy (above) Suburban anonymity map (opposite)*

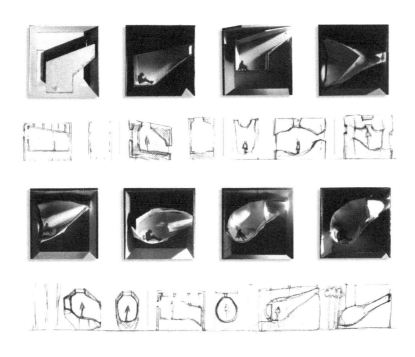

Stefan Dean *Individual sensibility: design
development models and sketches (top)
Nestling in Railway Fields section (bottom)*

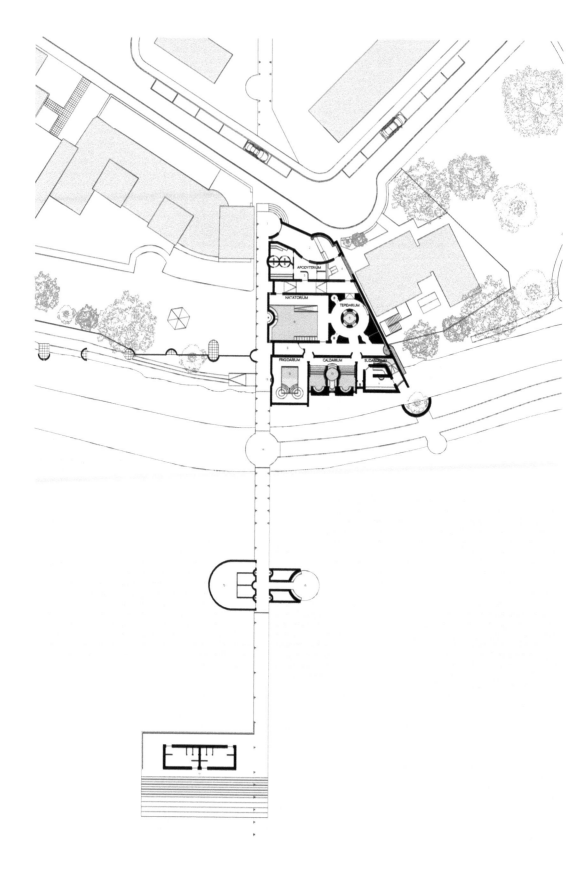

APODYTERIUM

NATATORIUM

TEPIDARIUM

FRIGIDARIUM   CALDARIUM   SUDATORIUM

GUY SINCLAIR
WEST RESERVOIR BATH HOUSE

The West Reservoir as an existing site of leisure, with open water swimming, water sports and nature watching, had to one side a ramshackle collection of NHS services housed in portacabins and hosts a yet-to-be inhabited semi-complete residential scheme. This proposal aimed to create new physical and thematic links between the reservoir, the medical facilities to the north and the New River walk.

The historic typology of the 'thermal bath' was studied and then used as a programmatic and formal starting point to develop a new hydrotherapy and rehabilitation centre for the NHS. This project was first conceived through the imagining and then detailed design of interior moments of inhabitation. The resulting plan as shown here, was one of a series of possible variations explored, which enabled the complex geometric resolution of bringing these moments together as a coherent proposal. Semi-enclosed spaces lit by skylights and using natural materials for human touch were connected with the bathing pavilion in the reservoir by a 'spine wall'. This also contained the complex building services and gave additional thermal mass to aide the regulation of the temperature differential between inside and outside in winter.

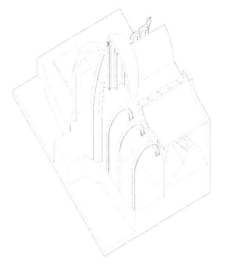

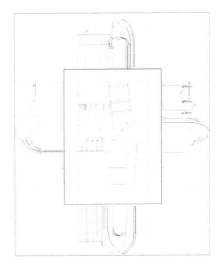

South Promenade: formalising the intersection between the two key axis of the site (above)

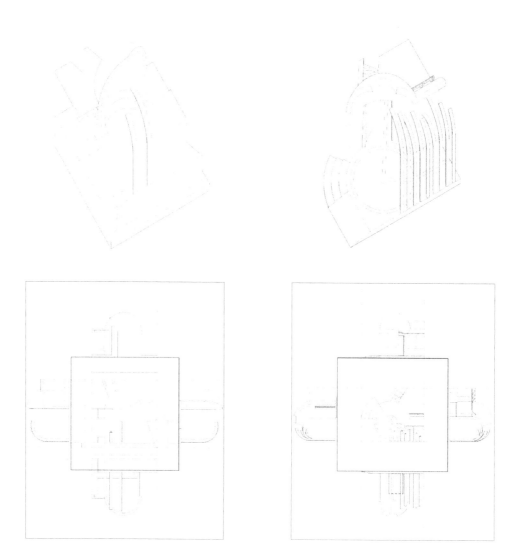

Guy Sinclair *North Seat: exploring the use of the dome to create a moment of repose, finding shelter and enjoying a view of the reservoir.*

South Atrium: developing further how a three-dimensional formal language can resolve and celebrate the intersection of fragmented volumes as partial enclosures.

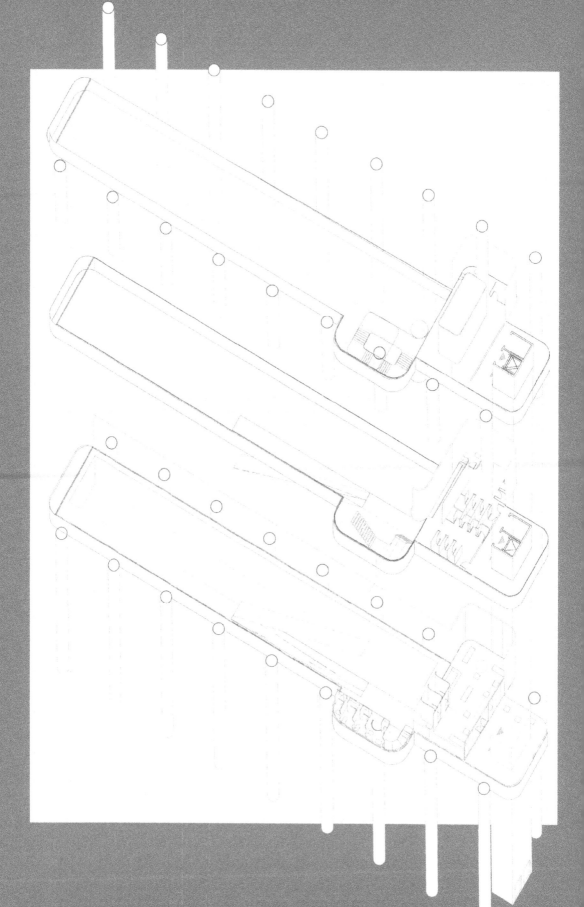

Located in Woodberry Downs at the edge of the West Reservoir, the new hydrotherapy centre looked to create a space that would, in addition to its bathing facilities, increase social interaction for the elders of Harringay and Islington. Initial research focused on what a routine visit to a health or hydrotherapy centre would be like for an older citizen. Key moments were identified, dissected and paired with one of the three distinct views from the site; encompassing the idea that nature and bodies of water positively effect mental and physical recovery.

The first space with a panoramic view of the reservoir, was proposed as an external recreational zone to be enjoyed by local residents and the wider community. At that moment, the building touches the ground and introduces itself to the visitors. The second space was the exercise swimming pool, with the user enticed to its end by the promise of a view across the water to the city. The third space was seen as a multitude of moments within the building, with the view interpreted as a human face; encounters which could occur at any time with visitors sharing conversations or a hot beverage. Connecting with each other and across to the external body of water beyond.

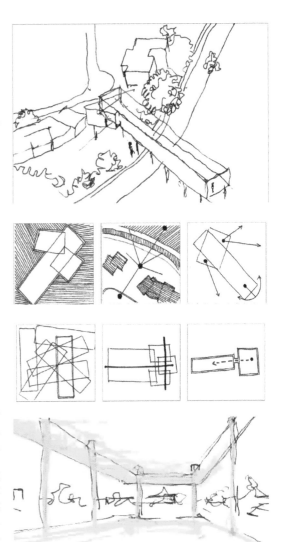

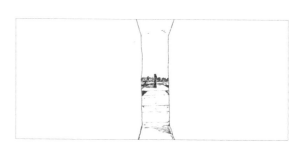

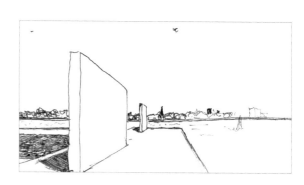

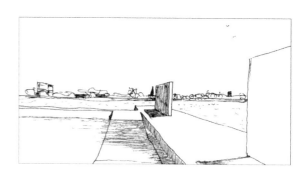

Development sketches exploring the potential journey through the (as yet undesigned) building and on to the new water's edge

PHILIP LONGMAN
THE WEST RESERVOIR, WOODBERRY DOWN

The Woodberry Down site sits within a peculiar nexus of ownership conditions, straddling a path owned by Thames Water but with a public right of way through it and extending into the reservoir. The reservoir was built as a private enterprise, then nationalised and now has been again privatised. The West Reservoir is currently owned by Hackney Council and leased to Greenwich Leisure as a water sports centre. Surprisingly however, public access to the water itself is currently prohibited.

The locale Woodberry Down is in the top 10% of deprived areas of the London Borough of Hackney. The number one cause of death in the Borough is lung cancer with much of the area failing minimum air quality levels. With the open space and vegetation in Woodberry Down there was an opportunity to improve public access and enjoyment to both the water of West Reservoir and the cleaner air of its environ. The main aims of this project were to expand inhabitable public space and to provide new hydrotherapy services for the local Cedar and Heron NHS Medical practices. Subsequently this would maximise local residents' enjoyment of proximity to the water and the fresh air, improving physical and mental wellbeing.

Scenographic model showing the parallax effect when walking the New River

"In ancient times the asylum was a space, often a religious sanctuary, where individuals could seek refuge. It was from these spiritual origins that modern mental asylums emerged. They became the places where Western ideas about mental illness were defined and different approaches to treatment evolved. Today asylums have largely been consigned to history, widely regarded as outmoded, inhumane and haunted places. Meanwhile mental illness is more prevalent than ever, and our culture teems with therapeutic possibilities." [1]

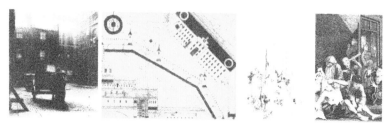

In developing your architectural programme for this semester's project, you will interrogate the original idea that the asylum represented – a place of refuge, sanctuary and care – and reflect upon how the provision of architectural spaces *including* a building to house a new charity headquarters[2] can respond to this idea and become a new **'civic cog'**.[3] The importance of sanctuary, knowledge and communication, rather than entrapment and isolation should be legible in your response to the brief. Both sites sit at the heart of their locale, enabling literal and metaphorical connections to physical and thematic contexts. These contexts will be defined and refined during your preliminary briefing process and will set the scene for your design work this semester.

A   **233 Albion Road**, Stoke Newington N16 9JT – headquarters for **'North London Cares'** [4]
    'North London Cares' is a community network of young professionals and older neighbours spending time together and helping one another in our rapidly changing city. This project will extend their operation from Camden and Islington to Hackney. Who are the 'young' and 'old' of Hackney and what activities might they do together to interact or to learn? What local concerns or incentives are there and what support services are offered by St Mary's Church and the Barton House Group Practice?

B   **Mitre Street / St James's Passage**, Aldgate EC3A 5DE – headquarters for **'Thrive London'** [5]
    'Thrive London' is an initiative set up by the Mayor of London with the NHS as part of their Healthy London Partnership aimed to improve mental health and wellbeing in the capital. This is currently a virtual endeavour run from London City Hall and implemented through small projects across London. This project will give the initiative a physical presence in the heart of the City of London amidst much ongoing development and a historical presence of the philanthropic endeavour of Sir John Cass.

---

[1] https://wellcomecollection.org/bedlam This Way Madness Lies: The Asylum and Beyond (London: Wellcome, 2016)
[2] we have selected two organisations for you to consider as your client, but are there others too?
[3] last terms' 'social hub' responded to local issues, whilst this terms' 'civic cog' aims to support city wide initiatives.
[4] https://northlondoncares.org.uk
[5] https://www.healthylondon.org/mental-health/thrive

16
17

REDUNDANT / REIMAGINED / CIVIC COG
SEMESTER 2

THE NEW RIVER: REDUNDANT / [RE]IMAGINED

Monifa Yasmin *Mappa Mundo,*
City of London

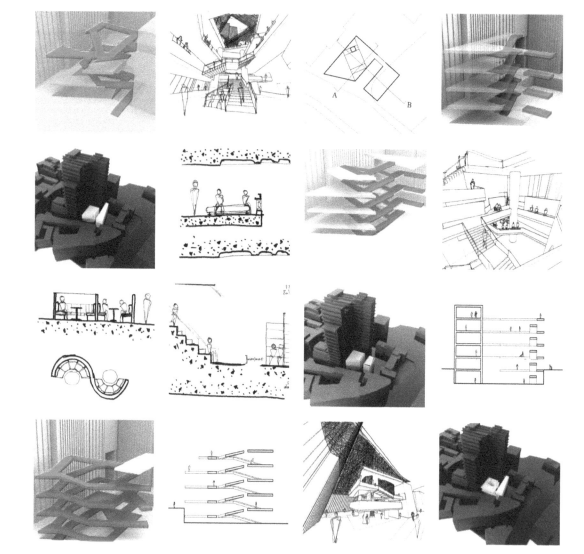

JOSHUA RICKETTS
THRIVE LONDON, AT MITRE SQUARE

Placing the new HQ for 'Thrive London' in Mitre Square, Aldgate, would bring conversations about mental health and wellbeing to the financial heart of London. Life satisfaction, feelings of self-worth and levels of mental health are below the national average across London, impacting people from all walks of life, from bankers to cleaners. The design of the building developed from an early vision that it should act as a device to enable a calm transition from public square to private talking booths, with varying degrees of privacy and different scales of space available for inhabitation.

The concept of 'problem solving booths' as put forward by 'Thrive London' was incorporated into careful furniture and niche design along the circulation routes, with a mix of warm tones from timber and coloured concrete dominating the interior.

The 'atrium' at the heart of the building touches the ground lightly, connecting with the existing sequences of urban spaces around the site and drawing passers-by up into the structure.

A netted façade was proposed to 'wrap' the building's form; encouraging the growth of plants on the south side to provide shade and greenery for the users.

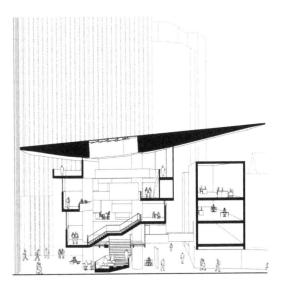

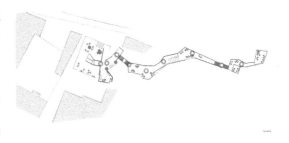

Section and unfolded plan (above)
Development sketches and models (opposite)

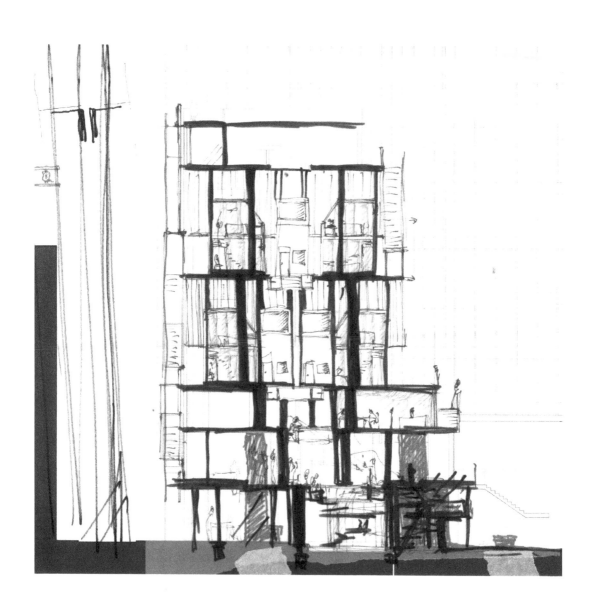

SIGNE PELNE
FINDING COMMON GROUND

'Search for Common Ground' is an existing UK charity focussed on challenging the way in which the world deals with violent conflict. This project aimed to bring their work to the City of London by offering a temporary refuge for some of the people impacted by the tearing down of their worlds; for those who might have been forced to seek a new life in a place perceived of as alien to them or where they do not feel they 'belong'. The idea of an 'inner sanctuary' forming part of an urban journey and as a semi-private space was the main driver of this project from the outset. This was combined with an initial architectural exploration of how physical space defines both our privacy and our connectivity with other people. The complex site in the City of London demanded careful consideration of pedestrian routes and its neighbouring buildings; from office block to church to school. The 'inner sanctuary' was later enhanced by the vision of vertical circulation as a journey rather than just a staircase; a 'village' like those of streets and squares. In its final form, the new 'vertical village' offered 16 mini refuges. The aspiration was that through an architecture enabling possibilities of interactions or privacy, residents might make new familiar bonds; in private and with others.

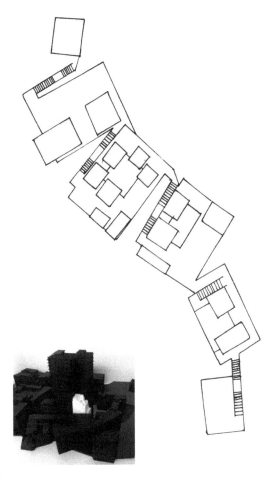

*Unfolded plan and modelled proposal in context
(above)
Development sketch section (opposite)*

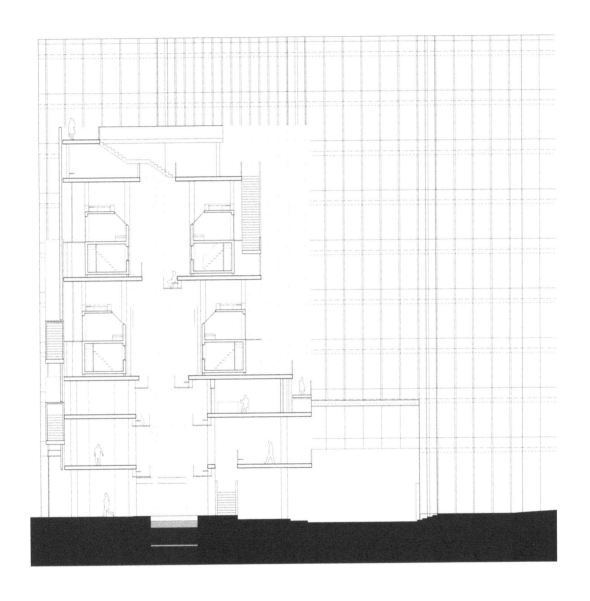

Signe Pelne *Section through atrium and vertical village (above);*
Development models and explanatory axonometrics (opposite)

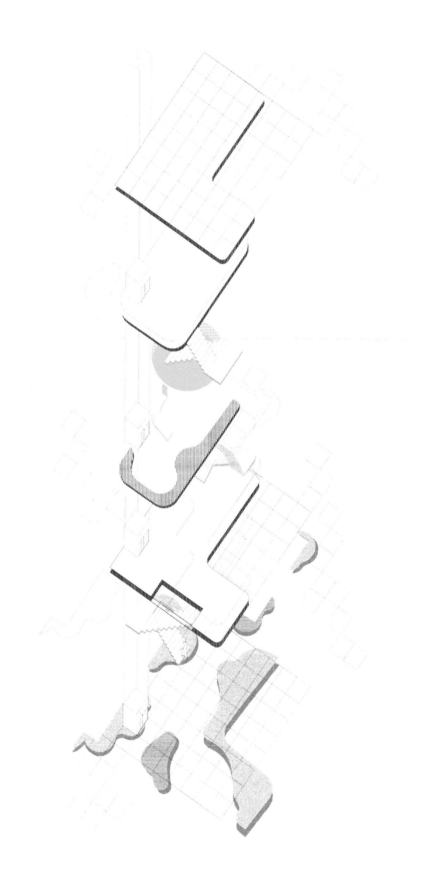

GADÉ SMITH
ADDA & EDEN, HQ FOR THRIVE LONDON

To define what a civic sanctuary might be in the centre of the City of London, research was carried out into the practices and ways in which therapy and wellbeing could be accommodated and achieved. The project was to be both a platform for dissemination and a physical space for people to inhabit. Conversation and face-to-face interaction can be used to enhance physical and emotional wellbeing; this is also known as therapeutic communication. The new building would not only provide spaces for the charity's management but would also house consultation rooms and various support spaces to help prompt conversation and encourage joint understandings. A large external public square on the ground floor with greenery provided visual therapy and street furniture to enable interaction and, perhaps, conversation. Cafés on the first and second floors offered places for spontaneous conversation between visitors over food and drink. A double-height space on the second floor allowed for public events or group talks. Whilst private or confidential discussions with professionals, nurses or counsellors were accommodated in a series of consultation rooms in the privacy of the third floor on the top level.

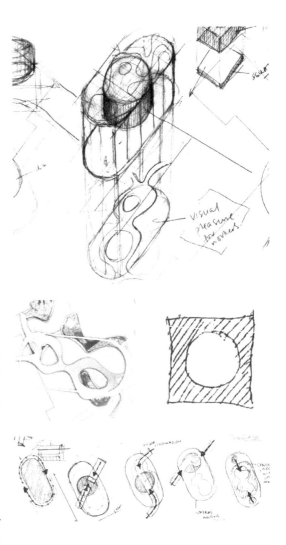

Development sketches (above)
Exploded axonometric (opposite)

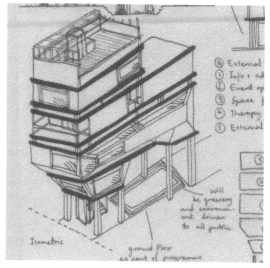

6 External
1 Info + ad
2 Event op
3 Space
4 Therapy
5 External

Will
be greenery
and environ-
ent driven
to all public

Isometric

ground floor
as part of programme

MONIFA YASMIN
A NEW HEADQUARTERS FOR THRIVE LONDON, ALDGATE

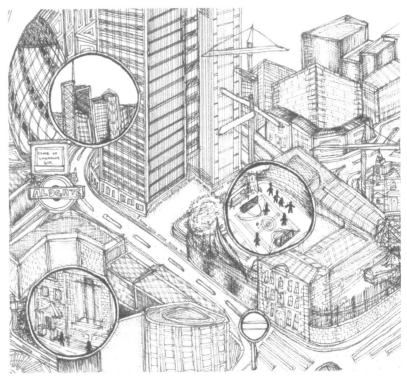

The dense, dark labyrinthine quality of the City of London was momentarily eased on this uneasy site in Aldgate. Mental health support services, counselling and a general wellbeing advice centre for 'city-workers' was proposed in response to the brief. City workers could pass by between the building's legs, or, if visiting, be lifted safely up into the building's underbelly. Inside, human-scale internal and external spaces offered privacy, anonymity and an escape from the outside.

Early site impressions (above top)
Iterative model and sketches sequence testing scale, solidity
and building programme (above and opposite)

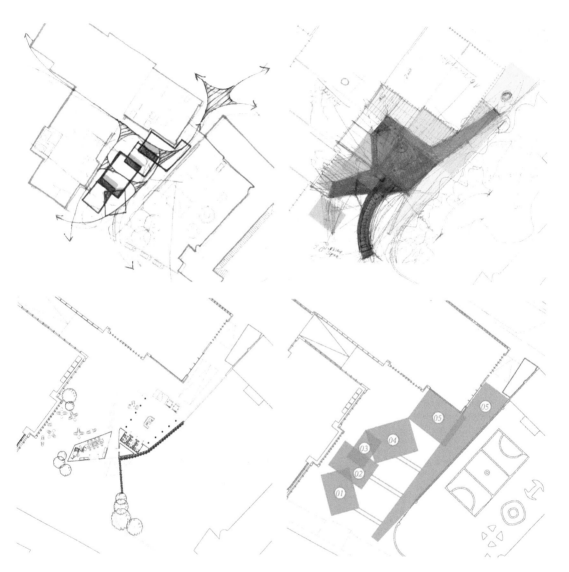

*Sketch development plans considering connective space
(circulation), inhabited space (pauses), loose landscape
(transitions)*

1 Publicity centre
2 Cafe
3 Book binding workshop
4 Library
5 Entrance space/ public route

ZUZANNA GRODZKA
BIBLIOTHERAPY AS THRIVE LONDON'S NEW HQ, ALDGATE

This new HQ for 'Thrive London' developed a programme in direct response to a careful study of what amenities one would typically expect in a London Parish. Each with their own church and designated priest, a 'parish' was a recognisable area with a sense of community. Everyday life was accommodated with, for example, places of worship and reflection, education, libraries and health support, community services and workshops. Gaps in provision within Aldgate were identified as including a community hall, library, and general spaces of spontaneous human interaction. These were then included in this proposal. Thrive London is a charity focussed on improving mental health and wellbeing. 'Completion of the parish' aimed to address ever-worsening issues of social isolation, work stress and limited time for reflection through inclusion of a new centre for 'bibliotherapy': book binding, library and reading places. Difficulties created by the tight verticality and complex boundaries of this site became a preoccupation in the resolution of this scheme through its plan. The proposal included exploration of in-between spaces and private moments of making, study or contemplation.

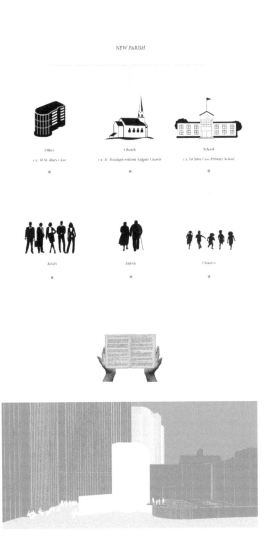

Preliminary brief definition and ghosted proposal

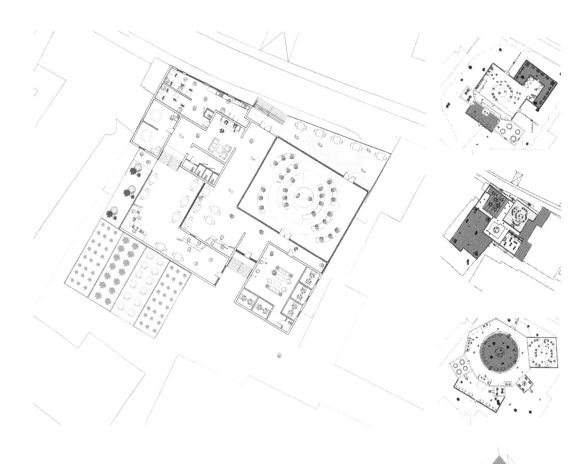

Jasdeep Atwal *Final plan and preliminary options (above); Internal images showing possible inhabitations (opposite)*

JASDEEP ATWAL
'TURNING POINT', LONDON

This project offered a new location and new building for the HQ of 'Turning Point', a drug and alcohol wellbeing service in central London. It offered facilities for people suffering with drug and alcohol abuse: one-to-one counselling spaces, group meeting spaces, and a communal hall were dispersed in the setting of a new garden centre facility. This was intended as a hybrid building for the city of London, offering new hobbies and cultivation of plants as a distraction from harsh realities and as a way of rehabilitation.

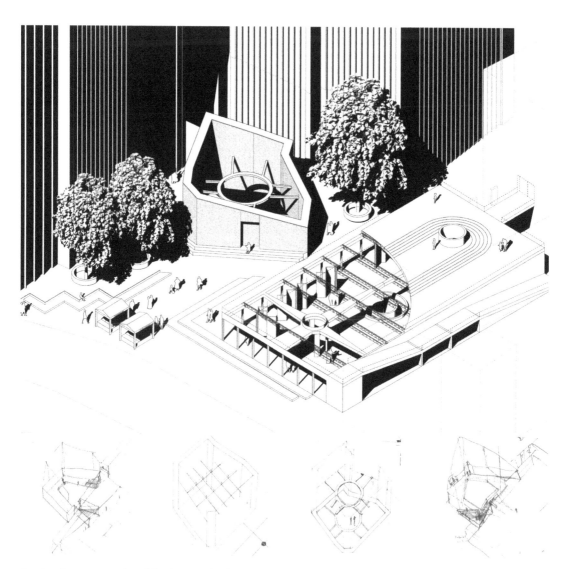

Construction axonometric and development sketches (above)
Early models testing inhabitation and spatial design (top, p.137)
Ground floor plan (bottom, p.137)

1 Hearing space
2 Administrative support
3 Problem solving booths
4 Digital server
5 Schoolyard given back to John Cass primary
school

PHILIP LONGMAN
THRIVE LONDON HQ, MITRE SQ.

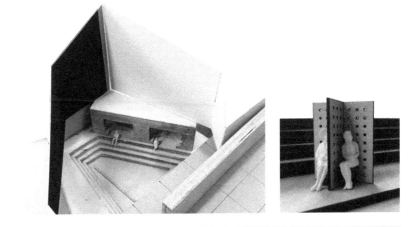

Thrive London is an initiative set up with the aim of raising awareness of mental health issues across London. Insight gained from interviews carried out by Thrive with people who have clinical depression and anxiety prompted the development of 'sky spaces'; spaces that 'feel buried' and 'like being under a duvet'; places for private reflection and to talk to someone. Architecturally, the intention was to provide a balance between openness and privacy; facilitating interaction, adjacency and conversation, as well as offering private places for support and advice services. A new public space for thoroughfare and festival at ground level connected down into the contemplative space and across to the PR event support offices.

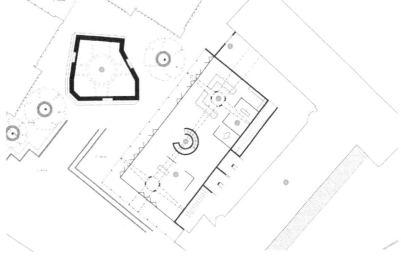

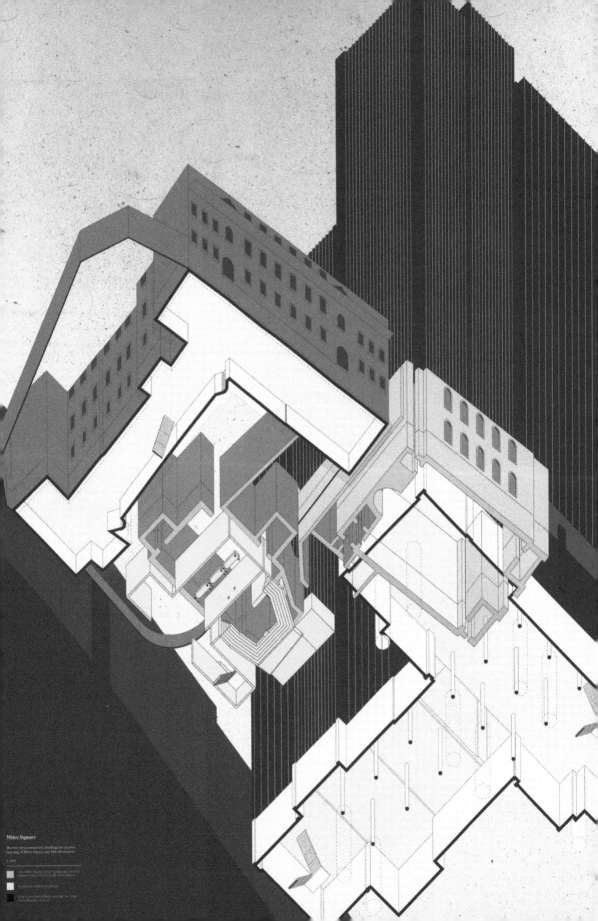

Mitre Square

Worm's eye axonometric detailing the current meeting of Mitre Square and Mitre Yard issues.

1 : 200

GUY ADAMS SCOTT BATTY
STEFANIA BOCCALETTI
STEPHEN BROOKHOUSE SAM
CADY FABIO CARDOSO DE
LEMOS CARVALHO DUSAN
DECERMIC JENNY DUNN
ELANTHA EVANS GEORGIA
FOLLETT AARON FOX JOHN
GRIFFITHS CLARE HAMMAN
DAVID HAWKINS KATE JORDAN
CONSTANCE LAU HWEI FAN
LIANG JAMILEH MANOOCHEHRI
ALISON MCLELLAN SARAH
MILNE NEGIN GHORBANI
MOGHADDAM NATALIE
NEWEY JOHN NG ANDREW
PECKHAM EMMA PERKIN
ANTHONY POWIS CLAIRE
PRIEST SHAHED SALEEM ANA
SERRANO JEANNE SILLETT
JACOB SZIKORA TSZWAI SO
MATTHEW STEWART OCTAVIA
STAN EMMA THOMAS
VICTORIA WATSON CAMILLA
WILKINSON SHUYING XU
FIONA ZISCH 2016-2017

Being an architecture design studio critic is a privilege. Invited to review the work of a studio periodically throughout the year, developments in the students' work are more evident that when the designs are seen on a weekly basis. It is only through the discipline of 'crits', where a student stands in front of an outsider to display and talk about their designs, that the student begins to master the languages of architecture. First, there is the graphic language, introduced in year one; drawing by hand or maybe digitally, creating a three-dimensional model, rough or perfected; creating an atmospheric representation of what a space may feel like, or how a design would transform the chosen site. Then, secondly, there is the lexicon of space and how to design it. This is perhaps where the unusual nature of the architecture degree is most pronounced. By the very nature of embarking on a course that has not been taught before higher education, the first year has to be heavily guided, introducing students to the skills and techniques needed to look at, design and communicate space. The interstitial second year has a necessary change in emphasis and tone. Design tutors take an important step back to give students the space to develop as designers; but, just like young fledglings, they often flounder at the start. This is where the third language of architecture, and perhaps the hardest to master, comes to the fore: verbal communication. As the second year progresses, one can see students growing in confidence. They begin to recognise the interplay between these three architectural languages; seeing which bits of a design might merit further development, assimilating the architectural dialect needed to translate and communicate ideas graphically to others and to themselves. Presented with the drawings and models a student has chosen to display, the critic helps to tease out and nurture areas of potential exploration and development that are implicit within the design, but the student has yet to acknowledge.

TUTOR REFLECTION
CLARE HAMMAN: DS(2)01 VISITING STUDIO CRITIC 2015-2018

ISHMA AHMED MUSTAFA AKKAYA ARISTIDES APATZIDIS JONES SADIE ALABBASI JASDEEP ATWAL ALEXANDRA BADEA DENISA BALAJ SABINA BLASIOTTI PATRICIA-CYNTHIA BOB IRINA BODROVA NAVPREET BOLINA MIA BRISCOE KATIE BROWN VERONICA CAPPELLI JEFFREY CHAN HANNAH CLARKE GEORGE COSBUC ELLA DALEY STEFAN DEAN ANA DIACONU THUONG DUONG YASEMIN EVMEZ MATTIA FARACI CHRISTINA GELAGOTELLIS KIRIL GEORGIEV DANIEL GLOAMBES ALLASTER GRANT ZUZANNA GRODZKA KATIE HAIGH OLA HJELEN CARLA HORA SABRAH ISLAM ANDREEA ISTRATESCU POLYAN IVANOV MANJOT JABBAL SOOYEON JEONG SHARNA JOHNSON MACIEJ ALEX JUNGERMAN DARINA KEANE SUSANN KERNER YASEMIN KOSE PHILIP LONGMAN BIBIANA MALAWAKULA NABLA MOHAMMAD FATEMAH MOHAMMADI YAHYA YIANNA MOUSTAKA AHMED MUSTAFA POLINA NOVIKOVA CLARISSA O'DRISCOLL ZUZANNA OSIECKA JAROSLAW OWSIANNY KYU SUNG PAI SIGNE PELNE NICKOLAY PENEV JOSHUA RICKETTS YARA SAMAHA SANDRA SIDAROUS GUY SINCLAIR ZUZANNA SLIWINSKA GADÉ SMITH CATALINA STROE GIA SAN TU SORAIA VIRIATO NABLA MOHAMMAD YAHYA MONIFA YASMIN YAGMUR YURTBULMUS ELINA ZAMPETAKIS TAMAS ZUBERECZ

00:47:24 Has anyone ever received formal training in any of the software they used at university, or was this done only in practice?

00:47:33 I have gotten the most training in practice yes. It made my experience working professionally very different from university because I used to do everything by hand. This is probably another example of the difference between what you learn at university and the realities of practice and, as a result, people go into practice thinking it will be more of the same only to realise it was not what they wanted and changed field. I know many people who have left practice and architecture because of this.

00:48:32 So you feel the disparity between the architectural teaching and what you are actually doing on the job is a problem as well?

00:48:50 Yes, it is

00:49:23 It was a bit of a struggle trying to balance learning the software with learning how to design. At one point, I was so focussed on how to use AutoCAD and Rhino that I forgot about nurturing my own design principles. And on the point of practice, it depends how lucky you are getting into a practice where you actually enjoy what you are doing. There are both small and big offices with so much range...some prefer to use Revit and others are stuck on CAD all day which, if you are used to working with mixed media in studio, can make you hate what you are doing. Luckily for me, I have such a variety and am also allowed to draw by hand.

00:50:21 Having read the book I thought more about second year studio and at the time I did not remember thinking particularly about the 'correct way of doing things' but now, looking back, the second year second term projects are the most resolved kind of

STUDENT REFLECTIONS

DS2(01) ON THE REALITIES OF PRACTICES: OFFICE AND UNI CONVERSATION TOOK PLACE VIA ZOOM 19 JULY 2020 thing that I have done within my four years of education so far. I remember just having conversations in studio, working through plans and sections and trying to convey information that was not just about achieving a finalised drawing which I think is very easy to get lost in.

And as to whether more focus should be given to learning the software: you see some studios that produce these beautiful drawings but actually what our studio focused on was the thinking process, which then allows you to get to that final outcome. It does not matter what the design steps are. The final production of drawing does not matter too much, it is more about the thinking behind it.

00:51:47 So you felt it was less about the aesthetic and more about the thought process?

00:52:00 Yes, it is actually quite difficult conveying that to a student though, when they are constantly surrounded by everyone else's drawings and look at the work submitted for medals as the style to aim toward. But if you get lost in the presentation, you lose the maturity of the concept and design.

00:52:18 You end up producing aesthetically pleasing drawings that lack substance.

00:52:26 Yeah for sure, and it becomes more difficult to justify when you start introducing the role of practice into the conversation of your overall education experience as well; it's weird because I want to teach but I suck at learning. I think I have learnt more in practice than the first year of MArch.

changed. Funnily enough, I used to never draw by hand but now it actually helps me think stuff through and convey information.

00:54:00 It gives you much greater freedom. But I guess it is something in the future that could potentially be lost. Even now, some people panic

MY METHODS HAVE CHANGED FUNNILY ENOUGH, I USED TO NEVER DRAW BY HAND BUT NOW IT ACTUALLY HELPS ME THINK STUFF THROUGH AND CONVEY INFORMATION

00:52:59 So do you think the education we get reflects life in practice?

00:53:10 For me at least, like others here, I was quite lucky. The projects were done on site and I quickly realised that understanding those practical processes were lacking at university.

00:53:18 It is a closer reality to what you are doing?

00:53:25 Yeah, and to go from something like that where you see the decisions you make reveal themselves in a very physical way, back to something that is completely speculative in MArch, I just felt like I was not working in the way I had done previously; my methods have

so much when their computer stops working.

00:54:40 Having returned to this more personal way of designing made me realise how good second year studio was at engendering that dialogue between design and the brief whilst asserting your individuality as an architect and designer.

00:55:06 One thing I will say looking back is that something that would have taken me two weeks to do takes half a day now!

00:55:17 We burdened ourselves in second year thinking we had to know so much, which you pick up very quickly in practice.

ILLUSTRATIONS

The study visit in 2016-17 took DS(2)01 to the plains of central Spain, where we were based in Madrid and made day-trips to Toledo (the 'city of three cultures'), Avila ('the town of stones and saints') and Chinchon (the village of bull-fighting and anis). In addition to urban walks and building visits in Madrid, we carried out more detailed urban studies of the three smaller, more easily comprehensible cities and towns. Through careful observation and different representations, drawing and mapping were used to explore the role of the 'plaza mayor' in relation to the town's spatial sequences and social life. The rhythms and rituals of the ordinary (everyday) and the extra-ordinary (festive) were evaluated in terms of how they might inform an architecture which creates a backdrop to foreseen encounters (programmed) whilst also supporting unexpected patterns of inhabitation (spontaneous).

The 'plaza mayor' is, for the 'old city', the centre of community life; a space for everyday encounters, for government bureaucracy, for festivals, spectacles, concerts, bull-fights, inquisition and even hangings! Students were also asked to consider how their use has changed over time? How are they seen today? Integral to local life, or a touristy stage set? What would these cities and towns be like without a 'plaza mayor' and its associated streets? What qualities do they bring? What is the relationship between governing powers and their manifestation in built form, the placing of institutional buildings within the city's fabric and how people use cities and inhabit space?

As an interlude between semesters one and two, the visit was intended to support semester two's design work, thematically and in relation to urban contexts and their possibilities.

16
17

INTERLUDE II: RHYTHM ANALYSIS PLAZAS PEOPLE

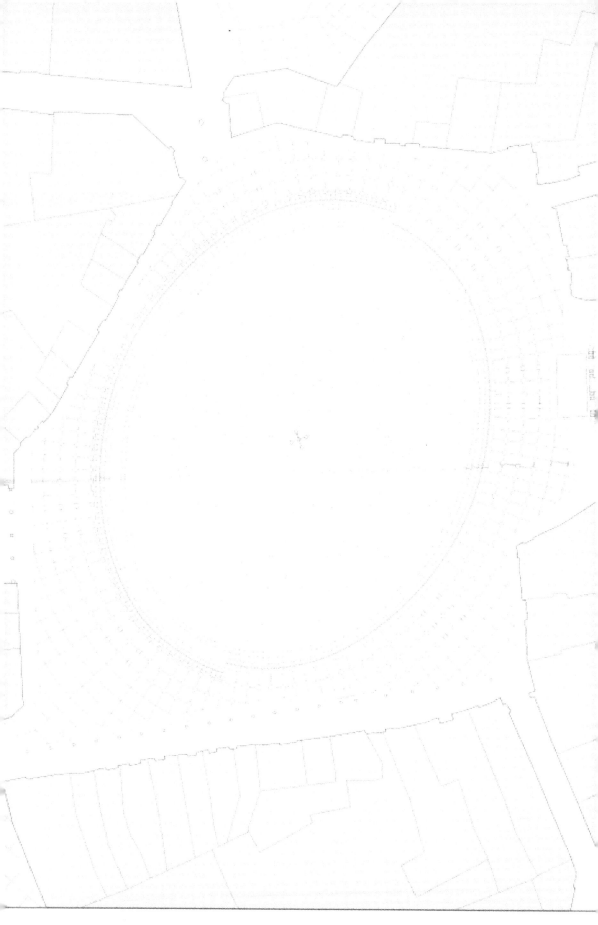

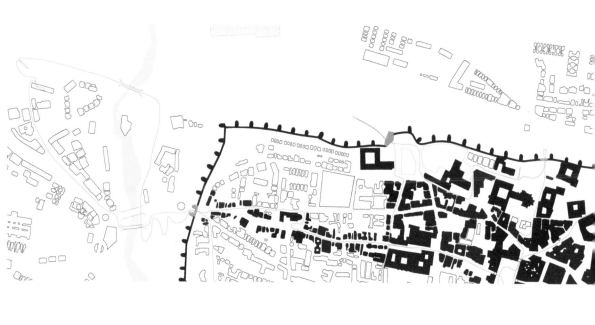

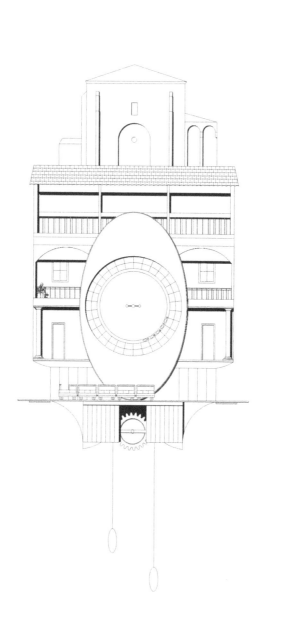

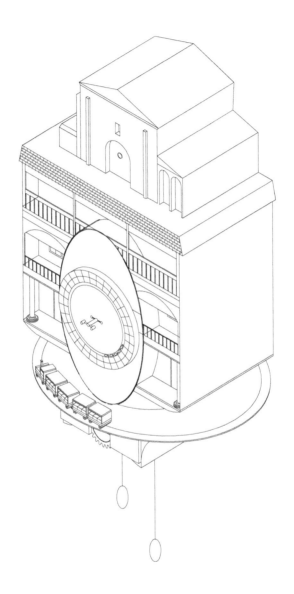

CALLE PINTOR MATIAS MORENO

PLAZA MERCED

CALLE COLEGIO
DONCELLAS

CALLE
ESTEBAN ILLAN

CALLE DEL ANGEL

CALLE DEL ANGEL

CALLE ALFONSO X
EL SABIO

CALLE ARCO DE PALACIO

CA
POZO AMA

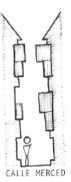

CALLE MERCED

TOLEDO VISIT 2017
URBAN SEQUENCE STUDY
ALEXANDRA BADEA
DS(2)01

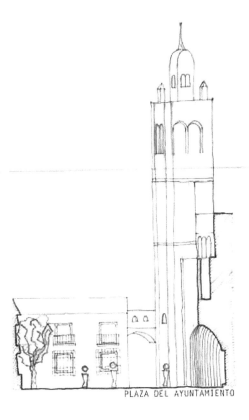

PLAZA DEL AYUNTAMIENTO

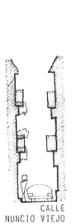

CALLE
NUNCIO VIEJO

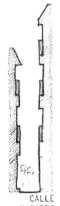

CALLE
NACARRO
LEDESMA

PLAZA DE DON FERNANDO

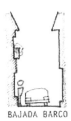

BAJADA BARCO

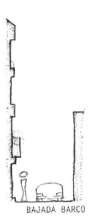

BAJADA BARCO

PLAZA MAYOR
RUTA MONUMENTAL
TEATRO LOPE DE VEGA

DS(2)01   ELAN

EVANS + DUSAN DECERMIC

17
18

A PUBLIC (IN)CONVENIENCE / DOMESTIC SANCTUARY
SEMESTER 1

A PUBLIC (IN)CONVENIENCE / CIVIC SANCTUARY
SEMESTER 2

A RIVER WESTBOURNE: [AT]TENDING TO CULTURE

ISHMA AHMED MUSTAFA AKKAYA ARISTIDES APATZIDIS JONES SADIE ALABBASI JASDEEP ATWAL ALEXANDRA BADEA DENISA BALAJ SABINA BLASIOTTI PATRICIA-CYNTHIA BOB IRINA BODROVA NAVPREET BOLINA MIA BRISCOE KATIE BROWN VERONICA CAPPELLI JEFFREY CHAN HANNAH CLARKE GEORGE COSBUC ELLA DALEY STEFAN DEAN ANA DIACONU THUONG DUONG YASEMIN EVMEZ MATTIA FARACI CHRISTINA GELAGOTELLIS KIRIL GEORGIEV DANIEL GLOAMBES ALLASTER GRANT ZUZANNA GRODZKA KATIE HAIGH OLA HJELEN CARLA HORA SABRAH ISLAM ANDREEA ISTRATESCU POLYAN IVANOV MANJOT JABBAL SOOYEON JEONG SHARNA JOHNSON MACIEJ ALEX JUNGERMAN DARINA KEANE SUSANN KERNER YASEMIN KOSE PHILIP LONGMAN BIBIANA MALAWAKULA NABLA MOHAMMAD YAHYA YIANNA MOUSTAKA AHMED MUSTAFA POLINA NOVIKOVA CLARISSA O'DRISCOLL ZUZANNA OSIECKA JAROSLAW OWSIANNY KYU SUNG PAI SIGNE PELNE NICKOLAY PENEV JOSHUA RICKETTS YARA SAMAHA SANDRA SIDAROUS GUY SINCLAIR ZUZANNA SLIWINSKA GADÉ SMITH CATALINA STROE GIA SAN TU SORAIA VIRIATO NABLA MOHAMMAD YAHYA MONIFA YASMIN YAGMUR YURTBULMUS ELINA ZAMPETAKIS TAMAS ZUBERECZ 2017-2018

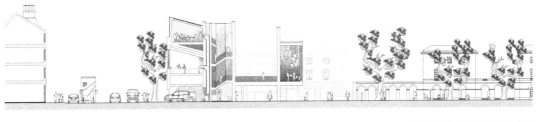

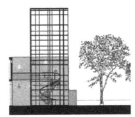

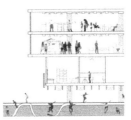

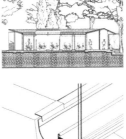

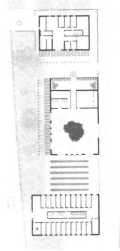

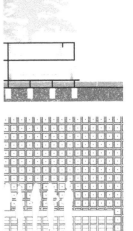

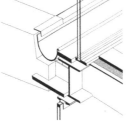

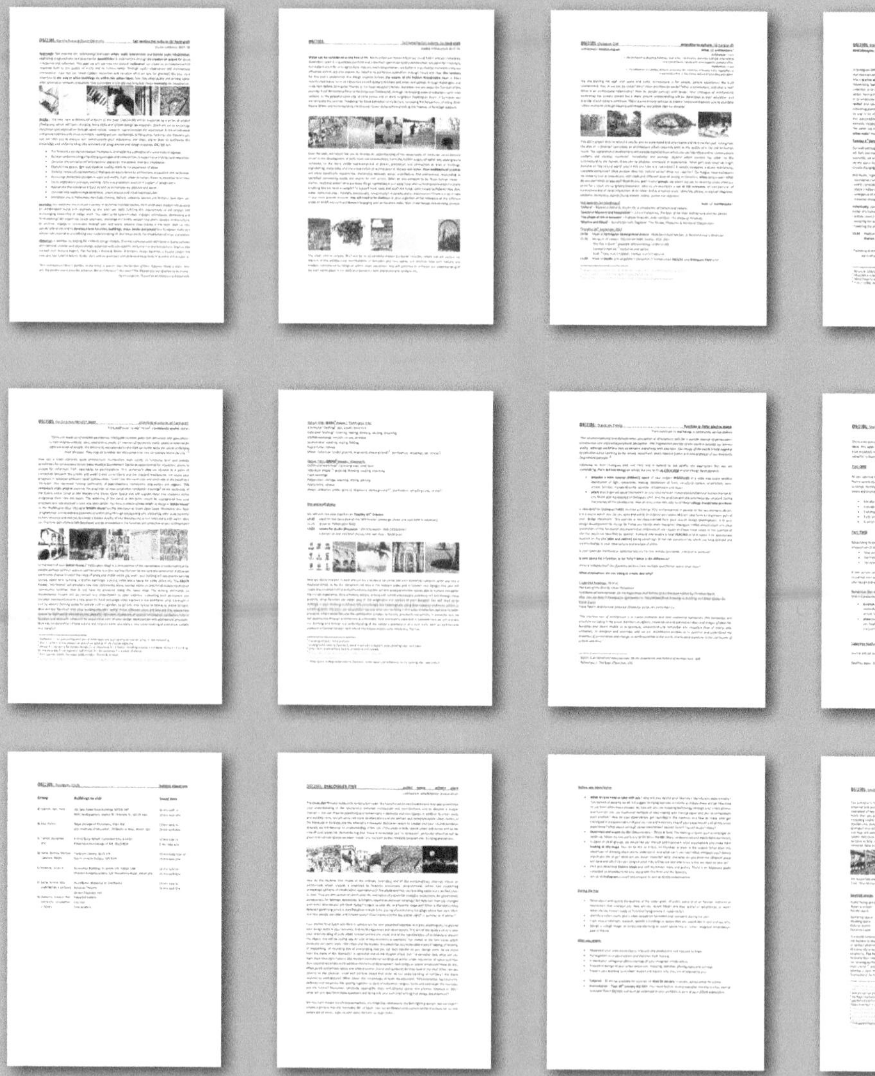

17
18

A PUBLIC (IN)CONVENIENCE / DOMESTIC SANCTUARY
SEMESTER 1

A PUBLIC (IN)CONVENIENCE / CIVIC SANCTUARY
SEMESTER 2

A RIVER WESTBOURNE: [AT]TENDING TO CULTURE

17
18

SEMESTER 1

SEMESTER 2

17
18

The hidden River Westbourne runs from Whitestone Pond to the canal-sides of Little Venice and Paddington Basin, then flows on through Hyde Park, down Sloane Street and past the Chelsea Flower Show, before finally greeting the Thames at Ranelagh Gardens. Ideas around 'cultivation' as manifest in architecture and society were explored; with horticulture and water considered as both resource and symbol.

[At]tending to culture: [a] hard graft. Proposal: from outhouse to our house / a new community service station. This project assumed the provision of new canal-boat moorings on the Grand Union Canal at Westbourne Green Open Space combined with a new heart for the local community. Wash-house: a re-invention of the launderette as a facility for people, perhaps without space or permanence, to clean and to wash. Green-house: a new local 'cultivation' hub for the allotments, nestled within an area full of established but hidden community facilities.

Interlude: studio study visit to Cordoba and Granada. Close attention was paid to the way in which institutional buildings sit within the urban fabric, how they effect public and private space and what presence (literal and symbolic) they have in the city. [SEE INTERLUDE I-III, P.67]

[At]tending to culture: [a] hard graft. Proposal: cultivation + propagation for healing + health. Proposal: a new charity HQ / a civic service station. This project proposed a new charity HQ, either for the Royal Horticultural Society or for the Trussell Trust. Envisaged as a new public-facing building with an architectural and civic presence, providing a new local facility and increasing public awareness of key issues challenging society today. Continuing with the year's theme of 'horticulture', the briefs, developed independently by students, responded to wider questions around self-sufficiency, provision of food, reliance on western medicines and increasing health inequalities.

17
18

A PUBLIC (IN)CONVENIENCE / DOMESTIC SANCTUARY
SEMESTER 1

A PUBLIC (IN)CONVENIENCE / CIVIC SANCTUARY
SEMESTER 2

A RIVER WESTBOURNE: [AT]TENDING TO CULTURE

"Cities are made up of invisible boundaries, intangible customs gates that demarcate who goes where: certain neighbourhoods, bars, restaurants, parks, all manner of apparently public spaces re reserved for different kinds of people. We become so accustomed to this that we hardly notice the values underlying these divisions. They may be invisible, but they determine how we circulate within the city." [4]

How can a small domestic scale architectural intervention both satisfy its functional brief *and* provide possibilities for connections across these invisible boundaries? Spaces as opportunities for interaction; places to escape for reflection; from passing-by to pausing-place. This semester's **sites** are situated at a point of connection between the (visible and used) Grand Union Canal and the (hidden) Westbourne, and locate your proposals in-between different 'local' communities: 'static' (on the north side and south side of the canal) and 'transient' (the east-west moving community of boat-dwellers, commuters, dog-walkers and joggers). **This semester's main project** assumes the provision of new canal-boat residential moorings[5] on the south-side of the Grand Union Canal at the Westbourne Green Open Space and will support these new residents whilst integrating them into the locale. The widening of the canal at this point should be incorporated into your proposals and represented in your site description. *You have a choice of **two briefs**: to design a 'WASH House' on the 'Paddington Stop' site, **or a 'GREEN House'** on the Westbourne Green Open Space 'Allotments' site.* Both 'programmes' aim to address questions of community through recognising and celebrating water as an essential human resource and ask you to reveal a hidden quality of the Westbourne or our relationship with water. How can this form part of the briefs developed and be embedded in the function and symbolism of your architecture?

At the heart of your **WASH House** / 'Paddington Stop' is a re-invention of the launderette; a facility essential for people perhaps without space or permanence, but also a place that can be the core of a community. A place we sometimes choose to visit? The ritual of going and of the 'while you wait'; your building will also provide bathing spaces, water tank re-filling, a clothes exchange, a public toilet and a space for water collections. The **GREEN House** / 'Allotments' will provide a new local community place, nestled within an area full of already established 'community facilities' that as yet have no presence along the canal edge. The existing allotments on Woodchester Square will be revived and embellished by your addition, supporting both permanent and transient communities with a new place for food exchange; what is grown in the allotments, what is brought in and by whom? Existing space for people with no garden, to garden; new spaces to retreat to, places to learn. How will the 'facilities' that your building provides 'serve' these different users and how will they create new spaces for both social interaction and peaceful reflection. Questions of cyclical inhabitation, symbolism, folly or function and aesthetic value will be explored as part of your design development and architectural proposals. How can consideration of how we use and respect water elucidate a new understanding of cultivation; socially and literally?

---

[1] *Outhouse*: 1 - an outbuilding with one or more seats and a pit serving as a toilet; privy; 2 - any outbuilding.
[2] *Our*: 1 - a form of the possessive case of we used as an attributive adjective.
[3] *House*: 1 – residence for human beings; 2 – a household; 3 – a family, including ancestors and descendants; 4 – a building for any purpose; 5 – a theatre or auditorium; 6 – the audience; 7 – a place of shelter.
[4] Elkin, Lauren (2016), Flaneuse, p286 (London: Chatto & Windus)
[5] https://www.theguardian.com/uk-news/2015/may/04/troubled-waterways-canals-london-housing-crisis-property-boats

17
18

A PUBLIC (IN)CONVENIENCE / DOMESTIC SANCTUARY

SEMESTER 1

A RIVER WESTBOURNE: [AT]TENDING TO CULTURE

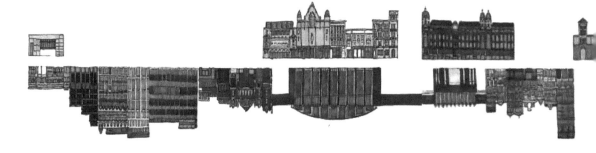

CAPTURING TERRITORY / MARKING MOMENTS

A preliminary mapping project (Dialogues One), took the studio on a walk from Farringdon to the Museum of London. Three exhibitions ('the city is ours', 'London's past air', and 'junk – one man's rubbish, another man's treasure') were visited and the half-day session was used to practice ways of seeing and mapping urban sequences and spaces. The territorial journey to start the year in 2017-18, began at the alleged source of the River Westbourne in Hampstead Heath and took us through the pools and follies of Golders Hill Park, south along its [sub]urban course, then stopping at the Westbourne Open Space where semester one's sites were located. There was time along the way to reflect on the contrast between the gritty urban east

London walk the previous week and how following the course of the River Westbourne expressed how water as a resource might impact residential areas; where buildings are situated and how urban densities subsequently develop. It was hoped that through this tracing, the histories of local communities could be uncovered and represented, with an emphasis on the role of the River Westbourne and its emergence through signs, symbols and physically through practical utilities along the way. These two samples of work explore the City of London's layers of materials, scales and building types from many centuries; with individual pieces of architecture standing alone, but also in combination giving an identify to streets and places.

Gia San Tu
Elevational study (bottom)
Urban mapping (opposite: top)

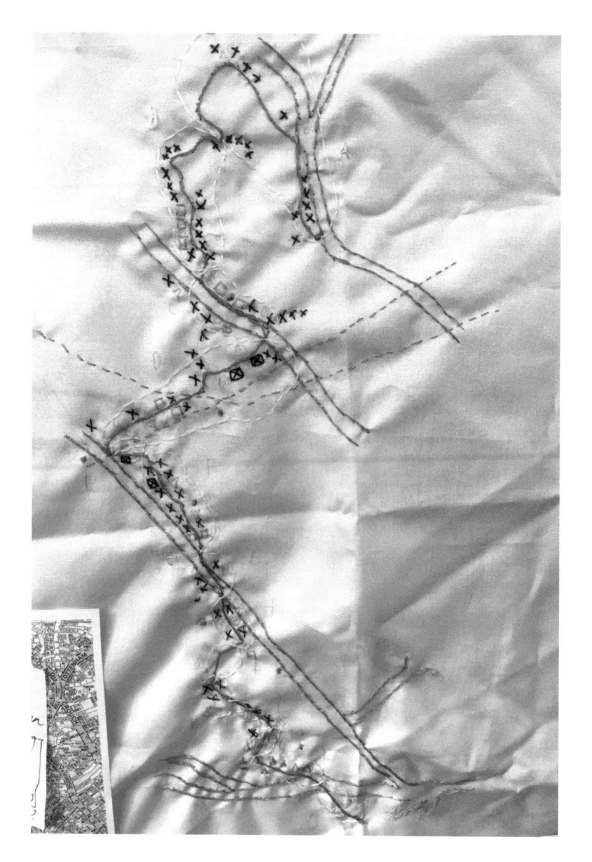

Ella Daley *Momentary impressions (above)*
Polina Novikova *Mapping, stitching (opposite)*

GIA SAN TU
A MODERN CLASSICAL
BATH-HOUSE

The site at Westbourne Green steps down in section away from the canal; interconnecting with a lower ground level to the north (new proposed market) and a higher ground level to the southern canal-side tow-path (proposed entrance and facilities for bathers). The design process was addressed in four clear strands; sequences of bathing, classical orders, expression of structure, and materiality. These had been identified following detailed precedent studies of, for example: the Caracalla Baths in Rome, the Duomo di Pozzouli in Naples with its vaults, the Corbera D'Ebre Church in Catalonia, Campo Baeza's offices in Zamora, and the Neues Museum in Berlin demonstrating clarity of structure and material. An internal ambulatory route acted as interstitial space between functions, levels, and light-solid/outside-inside, and became the main architectural driver in developing the 'final' design. The baths were centrally focussed on the first floor, whilst a light-filled, spacious, outward-looking roof laundrette room doubled as a place for reflection and 'passing time'.

Gia San Tu *Paddington Green site impressions*

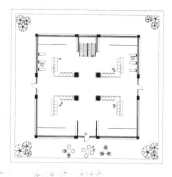

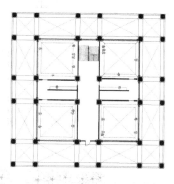

Gia San Tu *Plans, sections and elevations.*
A modern classical bath-house: the idea of an internal
ambulatory route later became a key driver for user experience
and the main challenge to solve architecturally in relation to the
four other strands of spatial sequence, 'orders', structure, and
materiality.

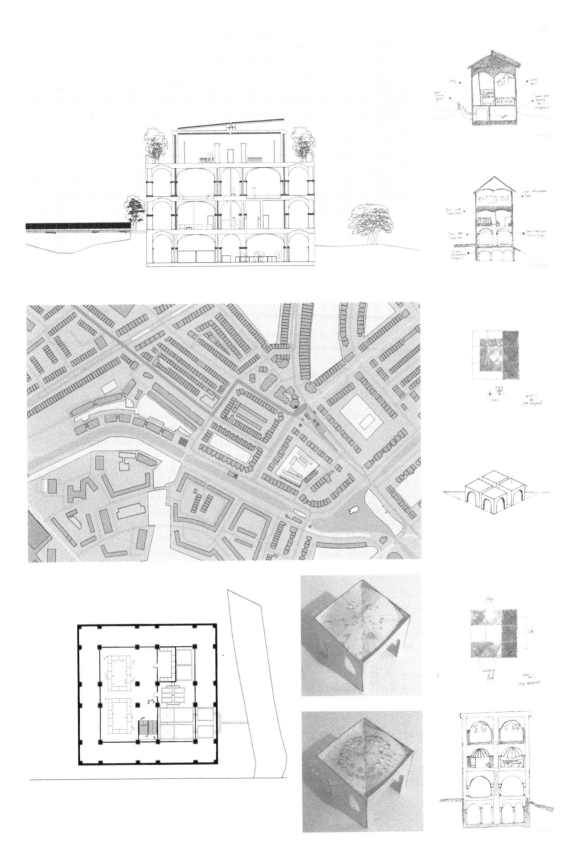

Mia Briscoe *Plan (opposite); Canal elevation (below); Rear elevation (right). The working process was dominated by designing through a series of hand-made cardboard models, exploring the proposal through horizontal layers, then through spaces, then through the layers again.*

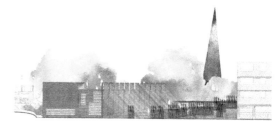

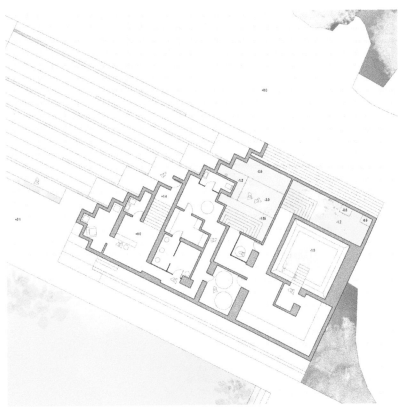

Should a connection across the level change in the site be attempted or should the new building 'give something back' to the local environ at each level; to the residential estate to the north and to the Grand Union Canal to the South? A public roof garden was proposed as a connection from the Canal, with a new sunken 'labyrinthine' bath-house below offering itself to the residential area.

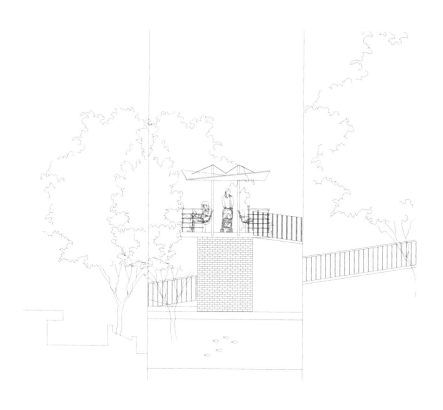

Nickolay Penev *New shelter for existing bridge (top and opposite); section through wash house and canal (above) sketchbook studies (pp.194-5)*

NICKOLAY PENEV
BOAT WORKSHOP + BATHING

A new 'wash-house' for bathing and laundry – a 'community service-station'. A café and boat workshop offered social and practical elements for both local residents and narrow-boat dwellers. Careful consideration was given to the canal edge; new promenade, wet dock, and a new shelter on the existing pedestrian bridge providing a place to pause and reflect.

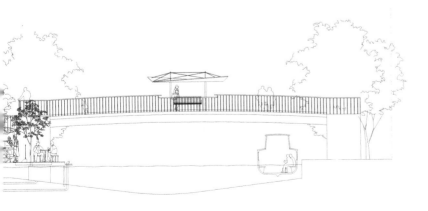

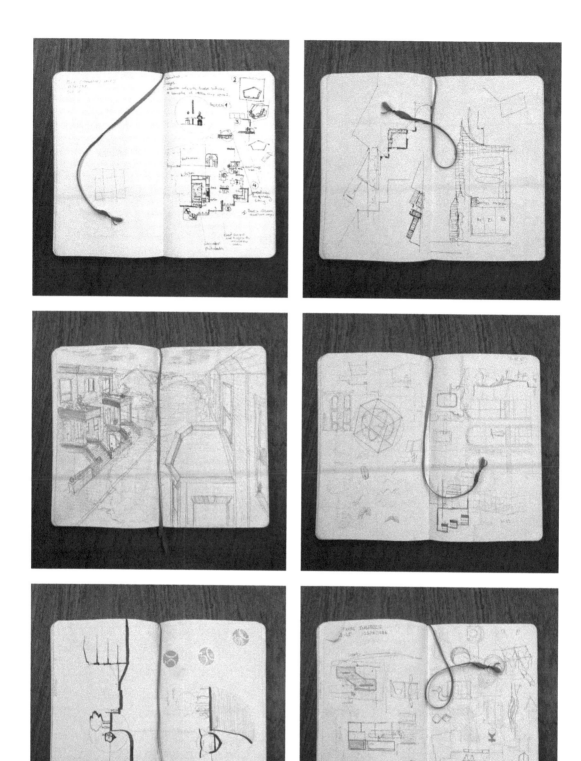

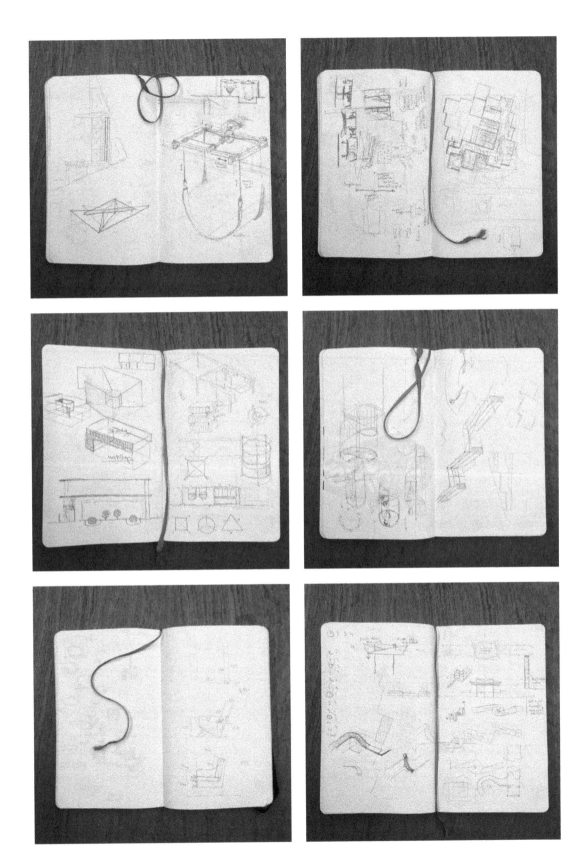

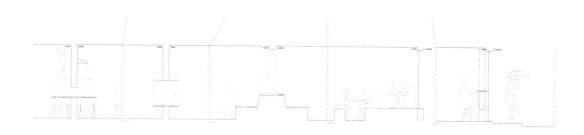

Nickolay Penev *Fold out section of inhabited spaces (above);
First floor plan (top, opposite); Long section through new boat
workshop, bathing and bridge link to Paddington Green (below)*

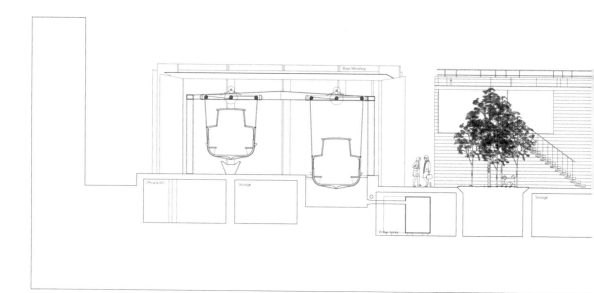

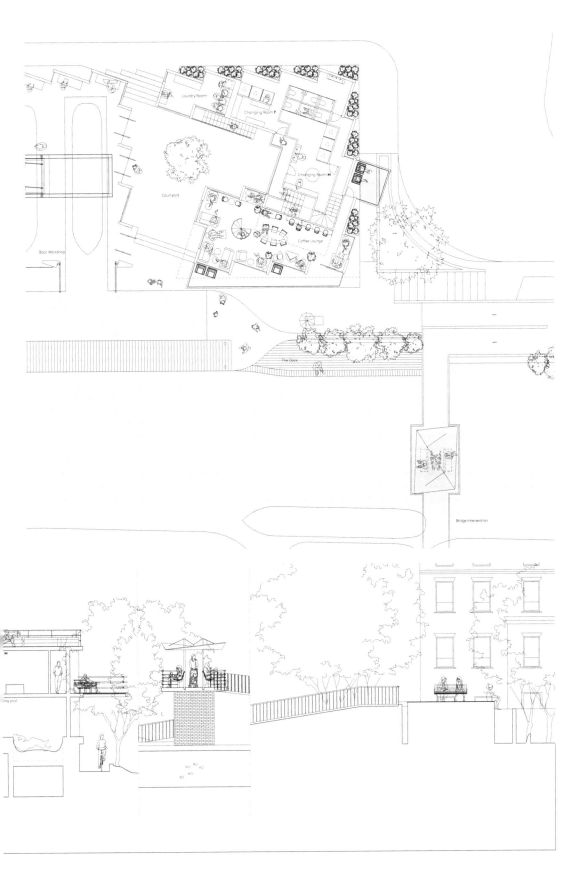

Laundry Room

Changing Room F

Changing Room M

Courtyard

Coffee Lounge

Boat Workshop

The Dock

Bridge Intervention

Swimming pool

Catalina Stroe *Construction and environmental services*
details shown on this section were developed as part of
the 'detailed design' carried out as part of the second year
Technical Studies submission

CATALINA STROE
WESTBOURNE GREEN MUSHROOM FARM

Careful site observation led to developing a programme to complement the existing allotments. A new mushroom farm with learning centre and water collection towers was proposed. Climatic requirements and the desire to keep the building single-storey resulted in a project with a dark, damp basement for the fungi to flourish. An internal walkway at ground level connected into existing routes through Westbourne Green Open Space. The plan is asymmetric, nestling in between existing trees.

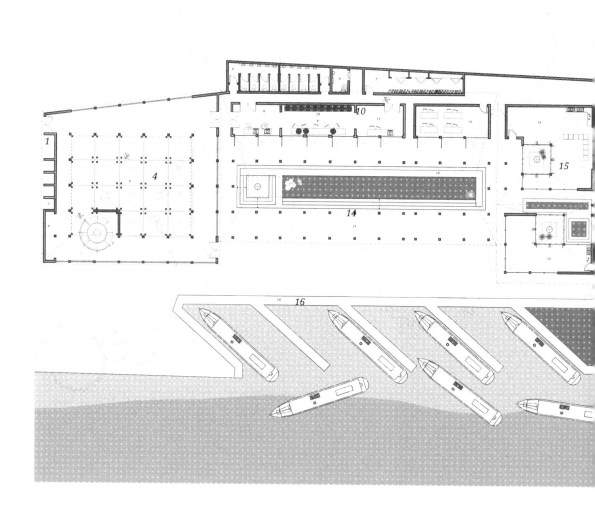

ZUZANNA SLIWINSKA
WESTBOURNE GROVE
ALLOTMENTS TIME FOR TEA

1 compost collection
4 tea growing beds
10 workshops
14 arrival arcade
15 tea houses
16 new moorings

ESSENTIAL UTENSILS
NEEDED TO PREPARE THE
TEA - BURNER, KETTLE,
LITTLE SINK

TAKING SHOES OFF T THE
ENTRENCE

TINY CUPBOARD IN THE
WALL FOR THE MUG
INDICATES IF THE SPACE IS
BEING OCCUPIED

This project aims to enhance the strength of the Westbourne Grove community by integrating the three user groups which make up the neighbourhood: ethnically diverse local residents, canal boat dwellers and passers-by on the canal tow-path. Tea drinking is taken as the shared cultural activity and tea cultivation as the new aim of the allotments. The programme is concentrated in three main areas: the tea farm, workshops for tea leaf preparation, and the more private tea houses.

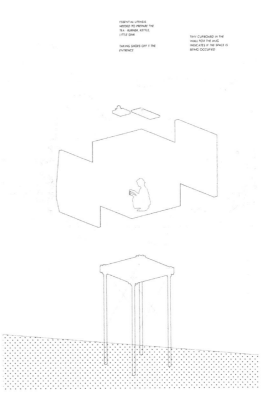

POLINA NOVIKOVA

SPONGE-HOUSE, LIGHT-HOUSE, FUN-HOUSE

A new 'social beacon' for the residents of Westbourne Green was proposed on this nodal site; transforming the mundane weekly wash into a space for self-cleansing and relaxation. Ode to Archigram!

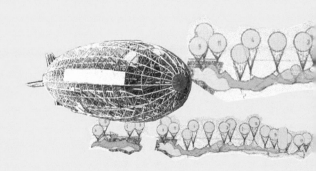

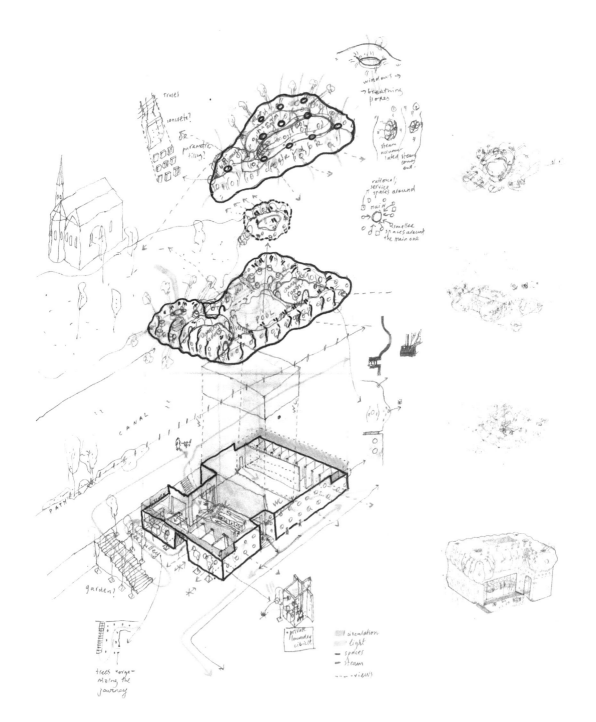

truss?

concrete?

δR

parametric tiling?

windows →

→ breathing pores

steam circulated steam comes out

rational service spaces around

main

smaller spaces around the main one

changing room

POOL

CANAL

PATH

WC

WC

WC

garden?

private laundry cibile?

trees *organising the journey

circulation
light
spaces
steam
views

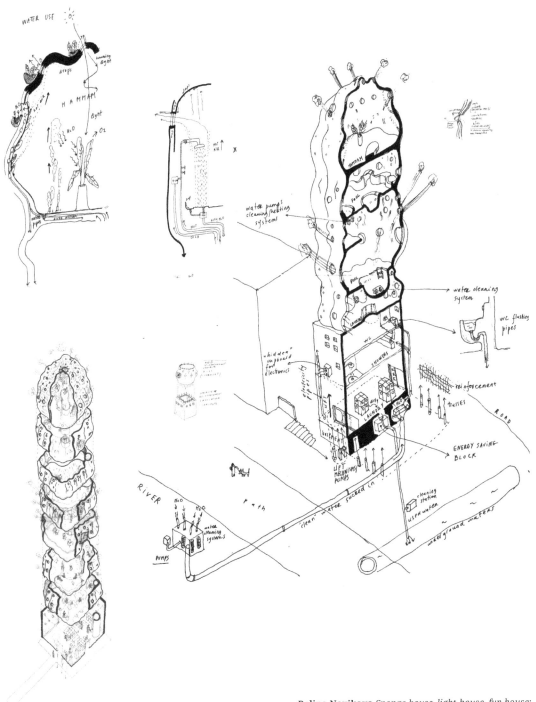

Polina Novikova *Sponge-house, light-house, fun-house:*
Brief and spatial development

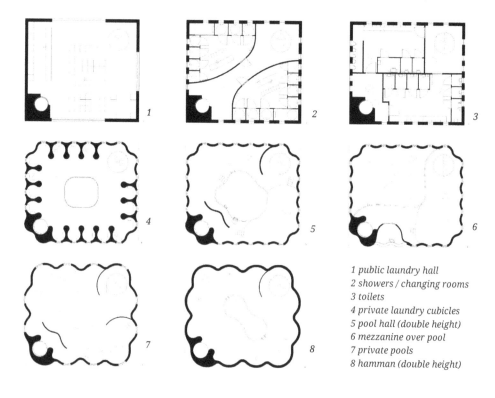

Polina Novikova *Sponge-house, light-house, fun-house:*
Site plan (above); floor plans (below);
axonometric (opposite)

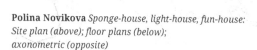

1 public laundry hall
2 showers / changing rooms
3 toilets
4 private laundry cubicles
5 pool hall (double height)
6 mezzanine over pool
7 private pools
8 hamman (double height)

This semester's main project asks you to design a new public-facing building which has an architectural civic presence and provides a civic service through a new local facility and through subsequently increasing public awareness of key issues challenging our society today. Continuing with the year's theme of 'horticulture', the briefs that you develop this term will respond to questions around self-sufficiency, provision of food and increasing health inequalities. The sites that you will chose from are situated at the end of the course of the Westbourne, close to where it discharges into the Thames. What have you learnt from our visits to Cordoba and Granada? How will your studies into 'thresholds', 'light' and 'inhabitation' inform your approach to architecture and how will water and celebration of the hidden Westbourne come into play? What can you take from an Islamic definition of 'paradise' as 'gardens, under which the river flows', and our ongoing consideration of function or folly, of aesthetic or necessity? It is intended that this brief is read in addition to those issued last semester. Now is a good time to go back, re-read and reflect on the broader context of the studio's endeavour.

We would like you to design either a new Headquarters for the Royal Horticultural Society or for the Trussel Trust. Your decision will be best made following site explorations and thorough research of subject and place.

	Royal Horticultural Society[1]	**Trussel Trust**[2]
Essential spaces:	A new HQ + 'cultivation' centre	A new HQ + 'propagation' centre
Public facing space:	market / fundraising / public education	market / fundraising
Water provision:	drinking fountain / bottle filing station	drinking fountain / bottle filing station
Private space:	'herb' garden[3] / 'water'	'kitchen' garden / 'water'
Gathering space:	lecture hall[4]	dining hall[5]
Working space:	workshops	teaching kitchens
Cellular spaces:	drop in advice RHS tips / apothecary	drop in advice CAB Chelsea / nutrition
Dynamic space:	seed bank / seedlings exchange	food bank / exchange

In a world dominated by international drug companies and an over-run NHS, this project assumes that **the RHS** has decided to develop a new set of workshops and facilities to improve public understanding of the possibilities of herbal / alternative / 'eastern' medicines.[6] The Chelsea Physics Garden[7] comes under the wing of the RHS and this new HQ re-invents and re-presents its benefits to support or counter modern habitual medicalisation of all conditions. **The Trussel Trust** works on the basis that 'anyone can reach crisis point'[8] and so they have decided to locate their new HQ in what is considered a rather up-market part of town. As part of their programme they run cooking workshops and hope to be a hub for charities addressing issues of hunger.[9] The facility will link into local church[10] and council[11] run food bank provision. Using the clues and links given, we expect to see you develop a clear thematic and programmatic brief which makes sense of place and space in the context of 'horticulture' for healing and health.

---

1 https://www.rhs.org.uk/education-learning/courses-workshops
2 https://www.trusselltrust.org
3 how are kitchen gardens, different from walled gardens, different from allotments? Derek Jarman's garden.
4 the Royal Institution lecture hall is a fantastic precedent, also other 'Royal Societies'
5 see Oxford and Cambridge colleges for dignified dining halls but consider events such as 'crisis Christmas dinner' and 'magic breakfast' in school holidays.
6 http://www.apothecarycentre.org.uk
7 https://www.chelseaphysicgarden.co.uk
8 http://londonfoodmap.org.uk/web/page/home
9 https://www.wscah.org and https://www.magicbreakfast.com
10 Chelsea Methodist Church, 155A King's Rd, Chelsea, London SW3 5TX
11 https://www.kcsc.org.uk/kc-p-n/food-banks

17
18

A PUBLIC (IN)CONVENIENCE / CIVIC SANCTUARY
SEMESTER 2

A RIVER WESTBOURNE: [AT]TENDING TO CULTURE

Nickolay Penev *A new HQ for the Royal Horticultural Society,*
King's Road, London. Elevation with Saatchi Gallery behind

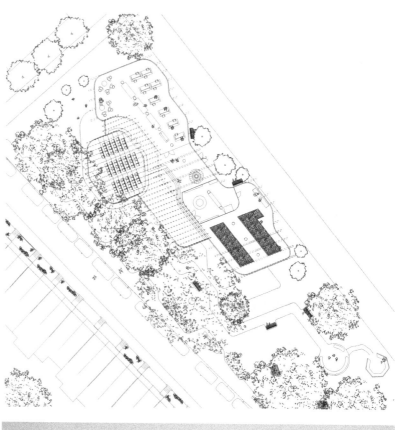

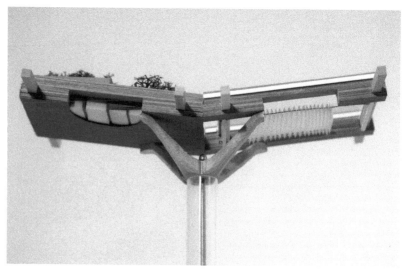

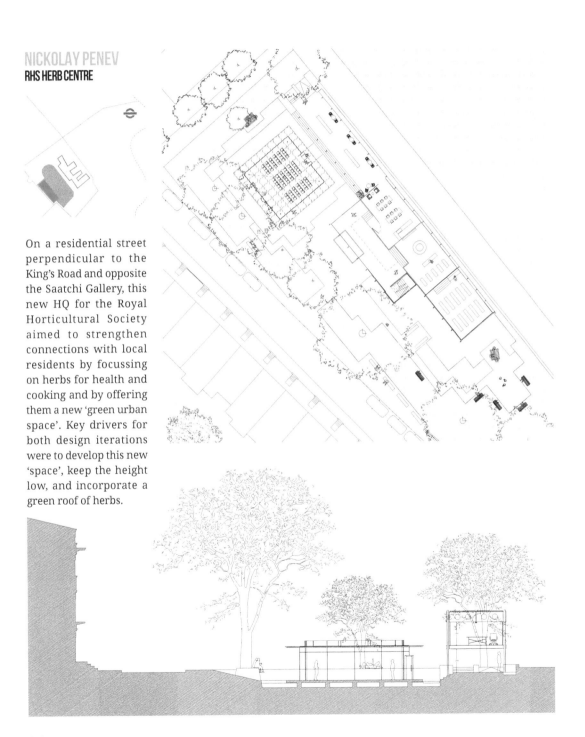

NICKOLAY PENEV
RHS HERB CENTRE

On a residential street perpendicular to the King's Road and opposite the Saatchi Gallery, this new HQ for the Royal Horticultural Society aimed to strengthen connections with local residents by focussing on herbs for health and cooking and by offering them a new 'green urban space'. Key drivers for both design iterations were to develop this new 'space', keep the height low, and incorporate a green roof of herbs.

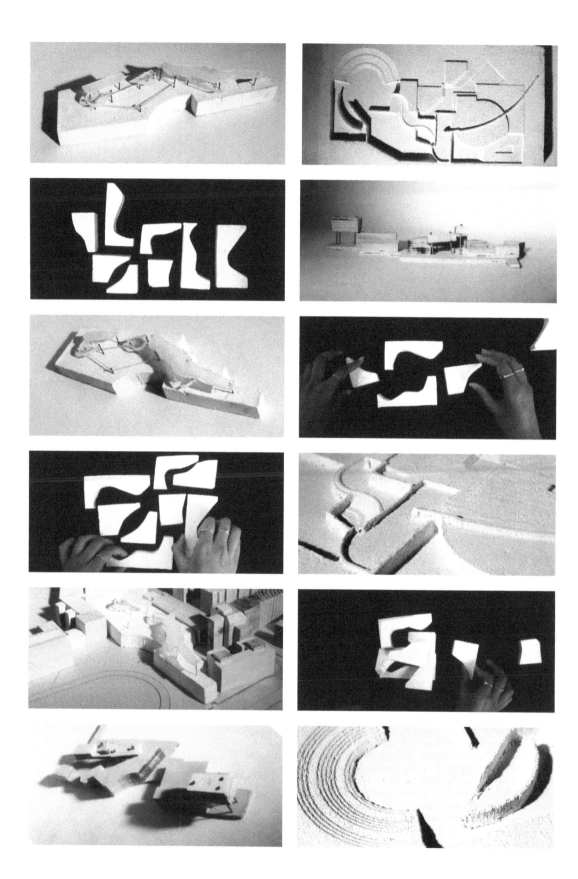

SABRAH ISLAM
RHS HEADQUARTER

After consideration of the possibilities of a new, visible presence for the RHS HQ as an adjunct to the existing Saatchi Gallery on the King's Road, the site chosen for the new building was to the south of the playing field, but a new proposed landscaping and planting showcase would extend into and ultimately replace it. Offering a new public meandering connection through to Chelsea Barracks and south towards the river and its new developments, the school's pitch was shifted to the west side and the running track integrated into the new gardens.

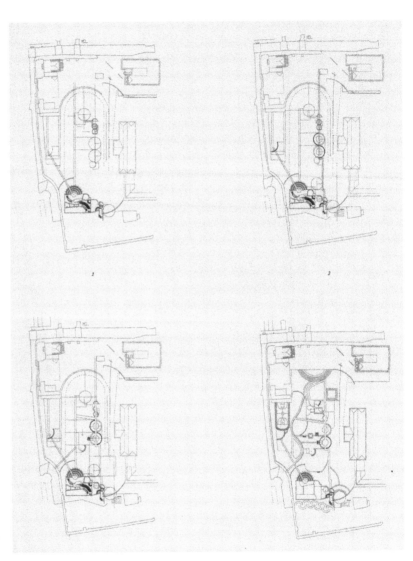

Sabrah Islam *Landscape scheme development*

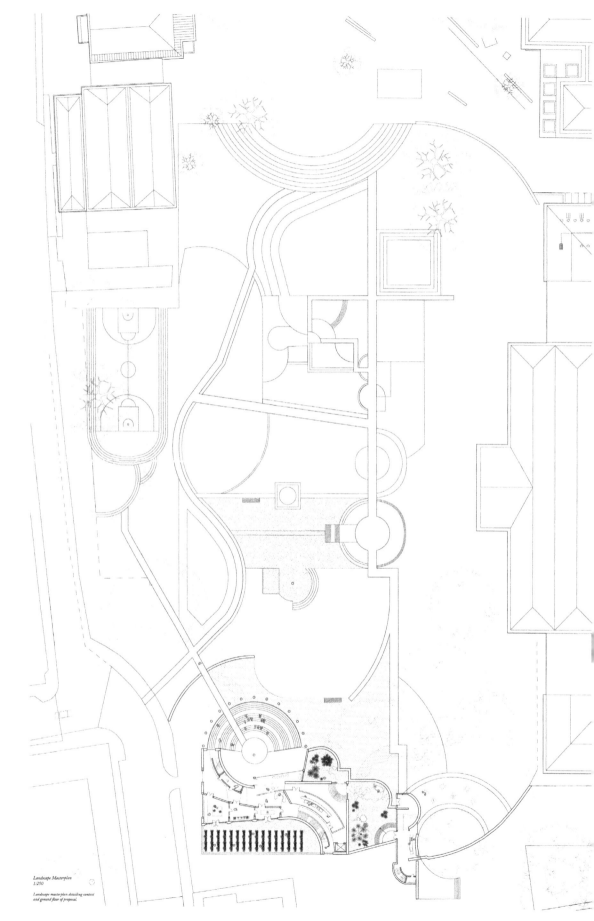

Landscape Masterplan
1:250

Landscape masterplan detailing context
and ground floor of proposal.

The proposal was developed in four layers; ground (engraving or relief), walkways (embed or elevate), walls (definition or connection), and roof (lighting or sheltering). A mix of hand-drawings and cast models were used to experiment with geometric forms to design a landscaping masterplan. Shallow excavation, or engraving of the ground created gardens of plants and water for contemplation, strolling and relaxation – also to showcase plant species for the RHS as a public exhibition garden. The building grew from carefully placed walls mediating between gardens and internal spaces, with roof forms as caps defining the enclosures and allowing a play of light on material.

Sabrah Islam *Masterplan in relief, hand-drawn (right) CAD drawn plan (p.216)*

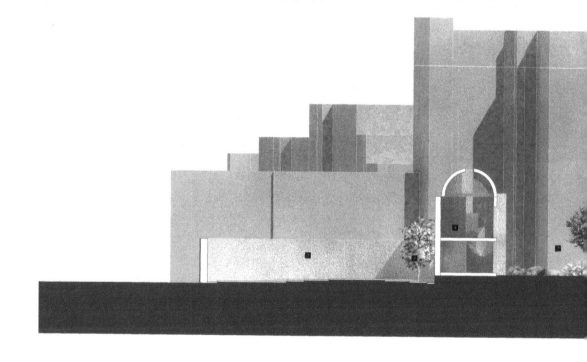

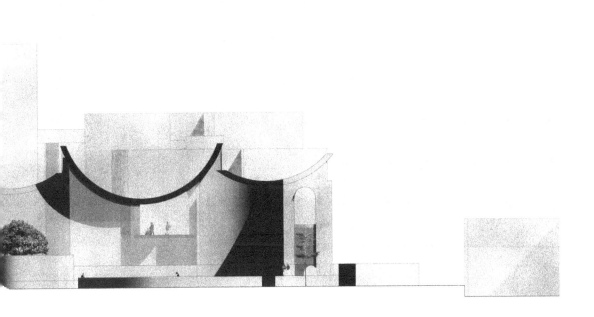

Sabrah Islam *Elevation (top) and section (bottom)*
Exploded axonometric (p.221)

ELLA DALEY
NATURAL HAIR CENTRE & RHS HQ

The King's Road, Chelsea was found to have a more diverse community than expected. However, hair salons did not include provision for the skills or products needed in the care of afro or asian hair. This project proposed a new inclusive hair centre with RHS greenhouse showcasing plants and herbs used in natural hair products.

Ella Daley *Building section (above)*
Preliminary development models (opposite)

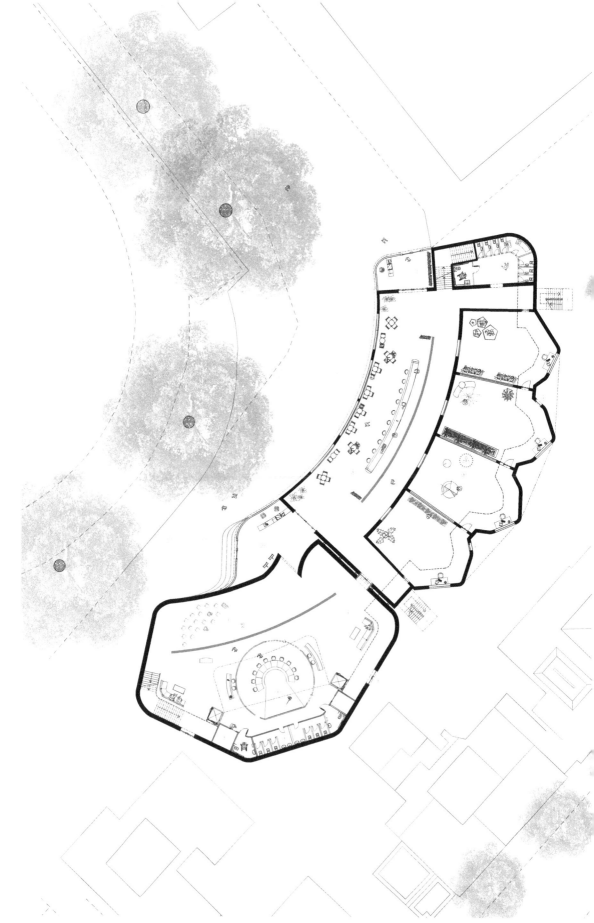

CATALINA STROE
RHS PLANT RESEARCH LABORATORIES

The site to the south of the Saatchi was chosen as it has a clear presence visible from the King's Road across the open green space, and ease of servicing separately from the rear. The intention was to pursue an expressive but articulated and organised architectural approach. Transitions and connections between public-facing areas, private laboratory and growing spaces have been carefully considered. Following many iterations to solve the tricky junctions and shifts between spaces, geometric resolution of this proposal was supported by a detailed study of the 'elephant house' at London Zoo.

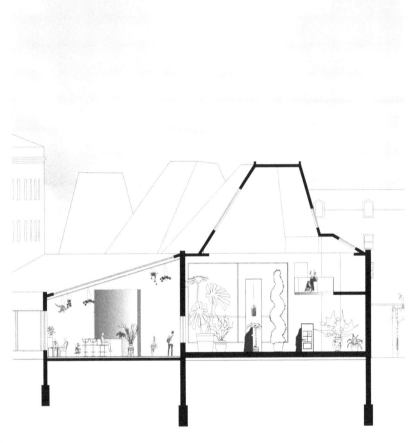

Catalina Stroe *Section (above); Ground floor plan (opposite)*

Katie-Anne Brown *Elevations and long section*

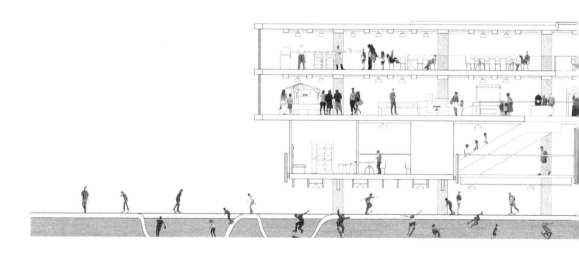

KATIE-ANNE BROWN
NEW TRUSSELL TRUST HQ AND COMMUNITY SPACE

The Trussell Trust HQ is brought to the heart of the King's Road to raise awareness of the food bank crisis and wealth inequality. Scale, materiality and colour; a striking contrast to the surroundings. The open ground floor plane welcomes skateboarders, before moving up into the belly of the building for community activities and up again to the food hall and dining space.

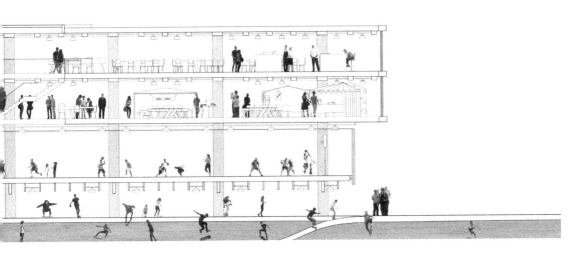

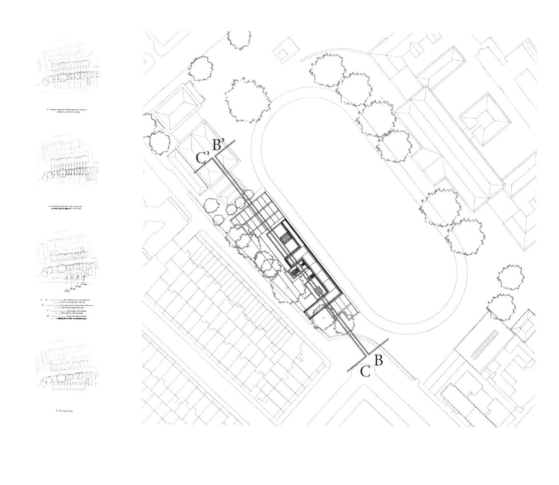

GIA SAN TU
HERB HOUSE: RHS TRADITIONAL CHINESE MEDICINE RESEARCH CENTRE

In the context of the ongoing medicalisation of many conditions and domination of treatments by pharmaceutical companies, this project proposes a new HQ and research centre for the RHS to promote awareness and benefits of Chinese medicine. One of the challenges of this site was to work out how to mediate between the scale of the residential street and the grand presence of the Saatchi Gallery opposite. To break down the scale of the new building and to respect and retain the existing trees on the site, a shifting grid was developed to help both the placing and the resolution in detail of the different architectural elements. The overall setting out dimensions of Herb House mimic the width of the Victorian terrace and protrude in three built forms amongst the herb gardens as the pharmacy, the kitchen, and the lecture hall and library.

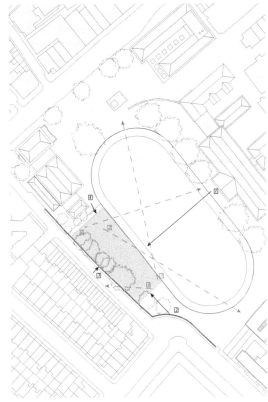

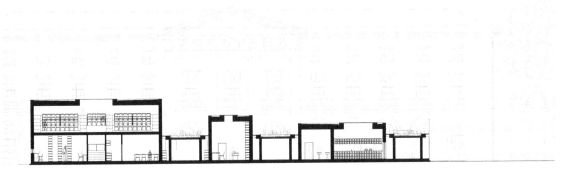

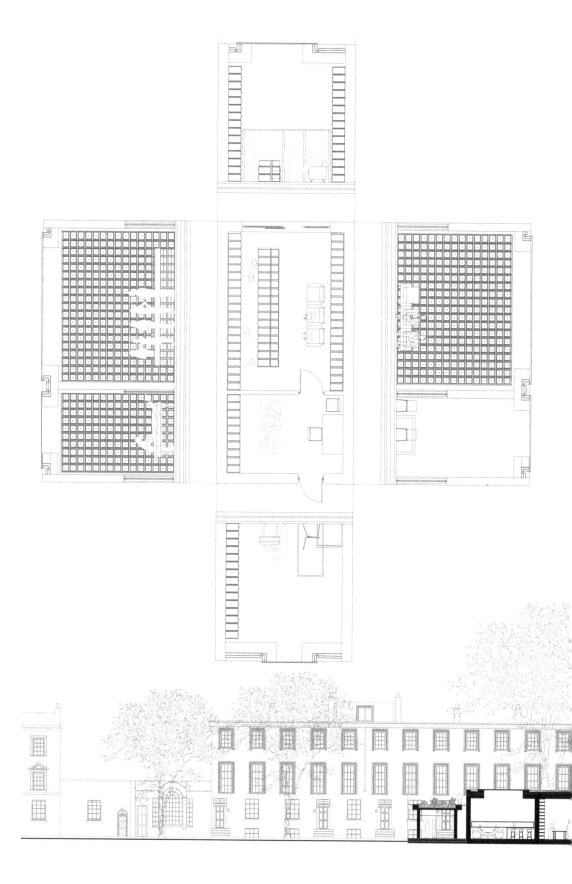

Each of the architectural volumes were designed from the inside out. From imagining the internal inhabitations and designing the furniture, to then ensuring that the solidity of the surrounding block allowed light in and views out as needed. The three main volumes protruded vertically through their lower, shared entrance and circulation spaces. The pharmacy volume with an adjacent consultation room was the first to be designed in detail (opposite). These design principles were further developed as part of the second year 'Technical Studies Design in Detail' submission.

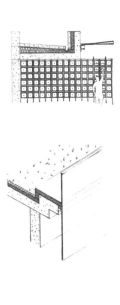

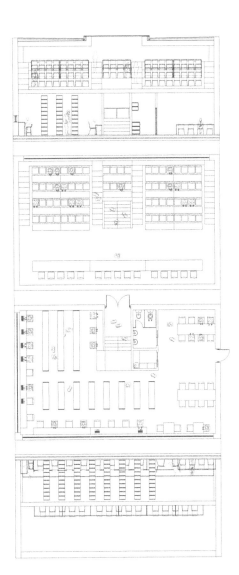

Gia San Tu *Fold out interior detailed designs (opposite and above); Long section through the three main volumes (below)*

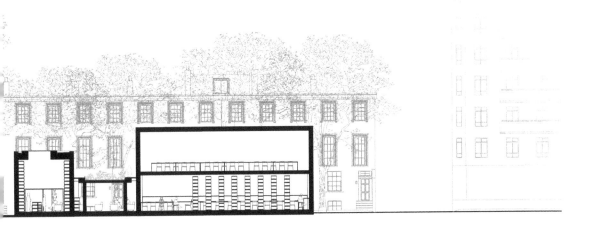

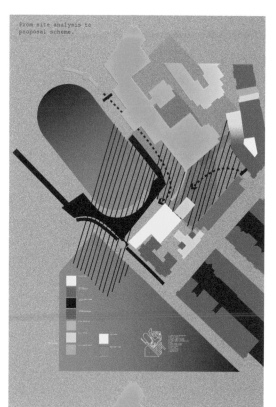
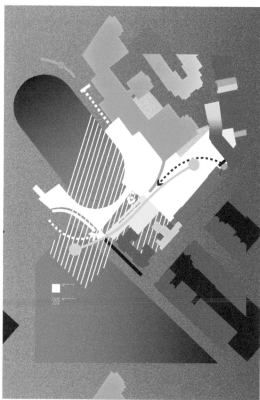

Polina Novikova *Contextualising the proposal: Uses and Connections*

POLINA NOVIKOVA
HORTICULTURE, APOTHECARY AND WELLBEING CENTRE

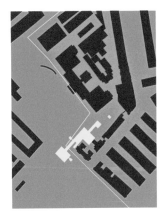

Linking the King's Road to the Chelsea Barracks to the south, this project proposes improving wellbeing through an apothecary-led horticultural approach to working with plants and people.

Polina Novikova *Axonometric*

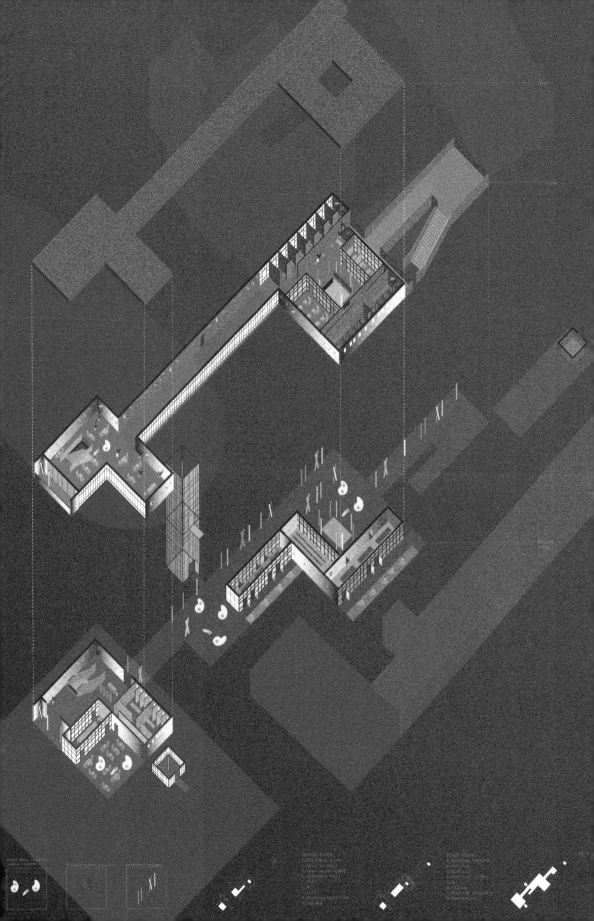

GUY ADAMS SCOTT BATTY
STEFANIA BOCCALETTI
STEPHEN BROOKHOUSE SAM
CADY FABIO CARDOSO DE
LEMOS CARVALHO DUSAN
DECERMIC JENNY DUNN
ELANTHA EVANS GEORGIA
FOLLETT AARON FOX JOHN
GRIFFITHS CLARE HAMMAN
DAVID HAWKINS KATE JORDAN
CONSTANCE LAU HWEI FAN
LIANG JAMILEH MANOOCHEHRI
ALISON MCLELLAN SARAH
MILNE NEGIN GHORBANI
MOGHADDAM NATALIE
NEWEY JOHN NG ANDREW
PECKHAM EMMA PERKIN
ANTHONY POWIS CLAIRE
PRIEST SHAHED SALEEM ANA
SERRANO JEANNE SILLETT
JACOB SZIKORA TSZWAI SO
MATTHEW STEWART OCTAVIA
STAN EMMA THOMAS
VICTORIA WATSON CAMILLA
WILKINSON SHUYING XU
FIONA ZISCH 2017-2018

We live in a world of inexhaustible choices, fed by hyper-production of objects – virtual or physical – whose only purpose seems to be to live a short life and produce a micro-dose of dopamine. These are complemented by a torrent of information bites, images swirling around in our peripheral vision. Surveying all this is a Herculean task; selecting, editing, responding now. It monopolises time like never before. Time measured in fractions of seconds, rather than days, months or years. Architecture has not remained intact; it is playing a part in this orgiastic neo-liberalist march to the precipice. It has opened its DNA to all kinds of processes of symbiosis, with some cross-pollination that has worked, but elsewhere it has created yet another hybrid that will not stand the test of time. While this abundance of new life is exciting, there is a danger that some fundamental knowledge, some critical values, have been lost. Architecture is a game of patience, a long game, one that needs to be built on solid foundations if it's to leave a meaningful impression. Part of this foundation is the drawing and reading of the plan, an orthogonal projection that has lost its primacy to the virtual or digital three-dimensional object, one that appears almost instantly, as if devoid of any attempt to pre-meditation. An architectural plan generated by any number of random slices seems, therefore, to be a resultant, incidental, unloved by-product. These fundamental pieces, however, one of type and the other of clear description, seem to be deeply unfashionable and disregarded within schools of architecture. Slowly we have succumbed to the lure of the instant, phantasmagoria; quotes and sensations all precariously glued together without any serious knowledge of formal compositions. An architecture studio, especially in the early formative years of a young architect, should restore the primacy of legible typologies as described in its written form of a plan with renewed urgency so we can recover what could be irretrievably lost.

TUTOR REFLECTION

DUSAN DECERMIC: DS(2)01 DESIGN STUDIO TUTOR 2017-2018

ISHMA AHMED MUSTAFA AKKAYA ARISTIDES APATZIDIS JONES SADIE ALABBASI JASDEEP ATWAL ALEXANDRA BADEA DENISA BALAJ SABINA BLASIOTTI PATRICIA-CYNTHIA BOB IRINA BODROVA NAVPREET BOLINA MIA BRISCOE KATIE BROWN VERONICA CAPPELLI JEFFREY CHAN HANNAH CLARKE GEORGE COSBUC ELLA DALEY STEFAN DEAN ANA DIACONU THUONG DUONG YASEMIN EVMEZ MATTIA FARACI CHRISTINA GELAGOTELLIS KIRIL GEORGIEV DANIEL GLOAMBES ALLASTER GRANT ZUZANNA GRODZKA KATIE HAIGH OLA HJELEN CARLA HORA SABRAH ISLAM ANDREEA ISTRATESCU POLYAN IVANOV MANJOT JABBAL SOOYEON JEONG SHARNA JOHNSON MACIEJ ALEX JUNGERMAN DARINA KEANE SUSANN KERNER YASEMIN KOSE PHILIP LONGMAN BIBIANA MALAWAKULA NABLA MOHAMMAD FATEMAH MOHAMMADI YAHYA YIANNA MOUSTAKA AHMED MUSTAFA POLINA NOVIKOVA CLARISSA O'DRISCOLL ZUZANNA OSIECKA JAROSLAW OWSIANNY KYU SUNG PAI SIGNE PELNE NICKOLAY PENEV JOSHUA RICKETTS YARA SAMAHA SANDRA SIDAROUS GUY SINCLAIR ZUZANNA SLIWINSKA GADÉ SMITH CATALINA STROE GIA SAN TU SORAIA VIRIATO NABLA MOHAMMAD YAHYA MONIFA YASMIN YAGMUR YURTBULMUS ELINA ZAMPETAKIS TAMAS ZUBERECZ

01:15:37 Having experienced crits both as a student and on the panel, it gave me the perspective of the role the tutor plays in your project's development which you were unable to grasp as a student. The mistakes that students make are always the same, so I can see why some tutors would force their students to adhere to a set of drawing or design rules. Do you feel that that is in any way beneficial to a student when you are bound by all these rules by a tutor regarding what makes a good design?

01:16:27 There are many layers to a question like that. The kind of 'house style' in a studio imposed by a tutor should not exist; I think a recognition of the diversity in a studio is better. I have seen (and probably the rest of you as well) someone on the verge of tears after a crit because someone has been awful which I find completely unnecessary and turns design into a joyless process.

01:17:00 Sadly an all too familiar sight in the architecture studio crits. Do you feel like critics and tutors should show more empathy towards the position of students then?

01:1737 Well, its a pedagogical thing. As a maths teacher now, I do not think you would eviscerate someone in your class when they are trying to learn.

01:17:45 Yeah totally, I try to find something good in every pupil in my class.

01:18:00 And I am sure you see a huge improvement in the students when you give them positive feedback.

01:18:11 Yes; once a student knows they can trust me, they then try harder.

01:18:17 So do you feel like the relationship is beneficial when there's mutual trust between a student and the tutor. Because, I mean, I

STUDENT REFLECTIONS

DS2(01) ON MENTAL HEALTH IN ARCHITECTURE EDUCATION
CONVERSATION TOOK PLACE ON ZOOM 19 JULY 2020

would agree that is the case within architecture at least.

01:19:11 It is important to give some guidance because it is very easy to approach the workload in an unhealthy way. No one stopped us and told us that it is not healthy to spend a week without sleeping and that is not going to bring the best out of you. I think having a healthy lifestyle whilst doing an architecture degree was difficult to come by.

01:21:08 Yeah, exactly, and that was a recurring theme. In architecture school, naturally everybody wants to do well unlike in some environments where you might need to encourage people with the method that they did. But here, you are investing a minimum of seven years of education to qualify, this is not an environment where pushing us to prepare us for practice was needed.

01:21:35 They wanted to be there.

THE KIND OF 'HOUSE STYLE' IN STUDIO IMPOSED BY A TUTOR SHOULD NOT EXIST; I THINK A RECOGNITION OF THE DIVERSITY IN A STUDIO IS BETTER

01:20:08 Did anyone else find that health was a problem? I mean personally, I can say I had moments where it was pretty bad, I do not know about anyone else.

01:20:19 I remember in first year, we had our first submission and almost no one slept and we all looked terrible. And the first thing they did was march us into the lecture hall for an introduction to Rhino seminar. It was like some kind of sick joke.

01:20:48 I remember, that could have been a great opportunity for them to set the tone for a sensible work ethic that contributed to a healthy lifestyle: have a nap, have a break.

01:21:02 You moved on to the next project so quickly that you didn't have enough time to recover.

01:21:37 Exactly.

01:21:40 Do you feel like in studios where you were negatively pushed to fulfil a particular criterion, you found yourself less enthused to work with them?

01:21:54 It did not so much push me away; it did not create the mindset which was good for moving forward. If you only have a hundred percent capacity and the body is being filled with worry, that's a part of my capacity that is not being used effectively.

INSIDE AS OUTSIDERS II

PART II : CONSCIENTIZAÇÃO

IN CONVERSATION WITH LAYTON REID, 21 FEBRUARY 2020

In the context of 'Dialogues and Dreams', this second conversation under the umbrella title of 'Inside as Outsiders' re-imagines the creative potential of conceptual understandings of 'the outside'. Instead of the idea of a thought 'from the outside', or the possibility of a 'pure outside' as perhaps including de-personalisation of the subject, inspiration is sought from another understanding of 'the outside' as an 'inside'; as a void or tabula rasa where diverse subjectivities can co-exist and thrive on the re-personalisation of the subject. In moving from Institute Benjamenta to Conscientização, what might the notion of being 'inside as an outsider' bring to ongoing enquiry into the 'role of the educator' in the 'cultural space' of the architecture design studio?

University, London, and through Desitecture (a research-based design group), he considers and produces solutions for the design of cities and their construction. These visions are based on applied research in poly-culture and the development of emergent technologies and materials; reconsidering the city as a responsive participant in society. Desitecture has presented, published and debated internationally. Layton is a champion of access to, and diversity in, architecture education and the liberation of the curriculum through internationalisation and the enfranchisement of the students' authentic contemporary experience of phenomena. He is currently creating a new diverse department of Architecture where he will continue to bring industrial

> ANOTHER UNDERSTANDING OF 'THE OUTSIDE' AS AN 'INSIDE'; AS A VOID OR TABULA RASA WHERE DIVERSE SUBJECTIVITIES CAN CO-EXIST AND THRIVE ON THE RE-PERSONALISATION OF THE SUBJECT

LAYTON REID is an architect, designer and educator. He was the founding Associate Dean for Architecture, Interior Design Environment Architectures and Urban Landscape Architecture at Ravensbourne

and societal aspirations together to advance the development of relevant and inclusive studies in architecture and architecture design; what are the future scenarios of the unasked questions?

ELANTHA EVANS is an architect, designer and educator. As a founding partner of Serrano Evans Partnership, design work brought together architecture, interior and object design and was occasionally balanced with the production of site-specific performances and installations. From early on, Elantha's practice work was punctuated with design studio tutoring. Commitment to deepening an understanding of the nature of architecture education began through teaching design studio and then by contextualising that experience in wider institutional structures with active involvement on RIBA Validation Panels in the UK and Overseas. Following the completion of an MA in History & Critical Thinking at the Architectural Association in 2013, Elantha's creative endeavour has since shifted more fully into the realm of architecture education and research. It has since continued in practice though the design studio, in module and year leadership, as an external examiner, and through study for a PGcert in Higher Education. Elantha is currently working towards a PhD in architecture education, exploring architecture education and the empathic imagination.

THIS INTERVIEW took place on 21 February 2020 at the University of Westminster. It was recorded with the permission of Layton Reid and then transcribed and edited by Elantha Evans for this publication.

EE *So I thought that we might begin our conversation today where Andy and I ended ours seven years ago*

with the architecture school as a version of 'Institute Benjamenta' learning, or being taught through 'de-personalisation' where the same things are repeated endlessly by people who are indistinguishable from one another in terms of the uniform, their skin, numbers... Without personal identity. In the 'bio' you sent me, you mentioned the idea of 'poly-culture' and of 'reconsidering the city as a responsive participant in society'. Perhaps this is something that could be expanded upon in terms of the educational as well as our physically-inhabited environment as something that might challenge the 'de-personalisation' of architecture education?

LR Things like 'Benjamenta' and this notion of never changing, anonymised delivery is in many ways the idea of education; that knowledge moves forward but is delivered equally to all, almost simultaneously and seamlessly. However, 'all' are not the same, and that's the thing that education has to deal with as not only products of our history but products of our experience, and although they are interrelated, they are not the same thing. If one isn't aware of those differences and isn't open to the possibility of learning from those things, what you have is essentially a repetition of the same, the same points of view. Science is starting to use artificial intelligence to do things like find a new kind of antibiotic by going through all the pathogens that exist and all of the so-called missed cures, to see if any of them when linked together can produce something else. What person is going to do that? Only someone who thinks from a different perspective, somebody who is prepared to re-investigate or re-consider the existing and look for new patterns. You can change the building but if you don't change the process what have you got?

LR I think there is a really big issue about what we value, because we seem to have a taxonomy of values in culture. What is legitimate? What is folk culture? We put a series of pronouns in front of these things to give a sense of where they sit on a map. This is a big mistake in a world

KNOWLEDGE MOVES FORWARD BUT IS DELIVERED EQUALLY TO ALL ALMOST SIMULTANEOUSLY AND SEAMLESSLY. HOWEVER, 'ALL' ARE NOT THE SAME, AND THAT'S THE THING THAT EDUCATION HAS TO DEAL WITH

EE *At the moment?*

LR At the moment.

EE *But if it is lost completely now, it will never come back. It is going already.*

LR What I mean is, shall we teach architecture students the realities of global building just because the chances are that is where they will end up? To train them for office duties? From those things, what you have is essentially a repetition of the same, again and again. The same sorts of rules, the lack of change, the same points of view.

EE *So, the stasis of repeated delivery reinforces education as knowledge transfer, but the crux of what we are really talking about is what it takes to create or invent culture; what produces culture in terms of our world?*

where materiality, waste, climate change and all of these things are changing the notion of what we think is 'culturally' appropriate. I don't think architecture even moves towards that, it tends to take a set line and an oppositional line. In the midst of all that it always fails to take into consideration that which is learnt from 'other'. So, let's introduce the notion of the 'outsider', the 'other'. What does that mean? If you have series of students who believe they own the cultural heritage, it is easy for them to build on something. They feel part of it. If you have a group of students who feel as though they are external and use the term 'I feel like', they can never ever say 'I do' or 'I am' so it is a metaphor for 'I am uncertain', 'I don't know exactly where I fit'. People will say 'I feel like that's not the way to go'; 'I feel like your attitude is'. 'I feel like' is almost a constant, a person in a constant state of uncertainty and uncertainty means they are unable to grasp or take part in some other kind of collective activity, such as architecture, not wholly. I suppose that notion in the liberal arts or humanities of a way of looking at language and applying that to our subject would release all of those considerations of experience, that those people encounter. Who are 'those people'? Often immigrants, let's be very straightforward about this, those who have not had access to higher education before and so do not know what to expect or don't know what the expectations of them are. Noam Chomsky might look at it in a socio-economic series of tropes which are defined by an understanding of how language controls or releases

as Stormzy was leaving his gym, he bumped into Prince William. Prince William said "Hi Stormzy", Stormzy said "Hi Prince". They inhabit the same ground; they have knowledge of the same kinds of peoples. One's interest is in the perpetuation of a particular system, and the other in the sending of a message and the raising of one's own personal circumstance.

EE *You raised the question of 'uncertainty of self' as one thing which creates a difficulty in expression and in declaring a stance or a position, but actually uncertainty as part of a design process or in terms of problem solving can be a positive, so if you*

BUT IN THE WAY IN WHICH WE TEACH, WE FIRST SAY 'YOU MUST BELONG' AND THAT IS KEY. IT IS THAT WHICH THE STUDENT FINDS DIFFICULT BECAUSE THE FRAMES OF REFERENCE ARE NOT AVAILABLE TO THEM

our capacity or possibility, and there are a whole series of writers like Toni Morrison – more prominent in America – who have an ability to articulate the pain and the sense of dis-establishment of such peoples. In the present, I think the creation of new languages or new kinds of opera – of which rap might be described as one – encapsulate certain kinds of thought and ideas very directly and links them to a personal journey that others can share. It is quite interesting how in this sort of popular culture, the notion of language and value is very easy to share amongst a very diverse group of people. I heard the other day that

are part of the establishment and not 'other', then your 'certainty of self' gives you the ability and freedom to then be 'uncertain' in problem solving.

LR I think the way in which it is couched normally is risk. In joining the system, one is taking a risk. The question is, as 'other', how much do you mediate your activity? When I say activity, I mean your response to design briefs and problems, as opposed to the initiation of a problem or brief, or the question of the nature of a project. The great fear for higher education and for the teaching of architecture is that the relevance of the 'classical project' will be reduced, that all of the principles that people hold dear will be eradicated. In that scenario almost anyone can own the possibility of production.

EE *To go back to your comparisons with opera and rap, the expression of thought through prose or poetry and the political side of that. Both the expression of self and the expression of a political attitude or something important to communicate – which you see in rap music – requires that certainty of self and fighting for it. But it requires practice, and failure. The UK Rap Game demonstrated this well. In a way that confidence, or that practice in clarity of communication that you see, is similar to what architecture students go through, but the media of rap is so much more direct that in a way I guess what we are searching for in architecture education is building that same sort of immediacy and confidence in everyone, but to understand that it is a process which has to be engaged with.*

LR But in the way in which we teach, we first say 'you must belong' and that is key. It is that which the student finds difficult because the frames

relation to what is accepted and what is the norm. A simple example in language would be a tutor asking 'would you like to pass me that cup'. To some students that is an indication of a need on the part of the tutor, but to other students it is a question, and the question isn't enshrined in the tutor but it is held by the person who is being asked. The response could be 'no I would not' – that is a legitimate answer but it is the wrong answer. The nature of the language which is used in the teaching of architecture is quite often pejorative, and alongside that it is dismissive of the values of other peoples' understanding of language. What happens then is you get architecture across the world which simply replicates the structural understandings that we have here in the West, and so we have a kind of sameness, a repetition.

EE *'Cultural products', in our case the built environment or its representation, tell us something of the work, the output, but not much necessarily of process or personality or individuality; not much of each person's unique cultural capital. There is then a question around how much that is*

THE NATURE OF LANGUAGE USED IN THE TEACHING OF ARCHITECTURE IS QUITE OFTEN PEJORATIVE. ALONGSIDE THAT IT IS DISMISSIVE OF THE VALUES OF OTHER PEOPLE'S UNDERSTANDING OF LANGUAGE

of reference are not available to them. So, you have a huge turmoil for students who are from communities which are culturally diverse in

deliberately oppressed or smuggled in or exposed, depending on who you are, in what context and in relation to what risk you are willing to take.

LR My snap response is that if you want to survive, quite often you have to be like the herd. If you don't join the herd, you are taken down by the lion. I think that is part of the culture of education. I don't mean that all tutors are like this but that they are bound by their traditions and their situation. It has taken us how long to get to the point where people can do visual dissertations?

of code making and the re-making of codes, pursued in many ways because I suppose people have to have a way of getting some kind of purchase on the system that governs them, and acting on that system. But if you look at these parallels, you can see that there has always been this need to communicate your cultural reference, your issues, your hopes, your sense of morality. In architecture we have a very similar

THERE HAS ALWAYS BEEN A NEED TO COMMUNICATE YOUR CULTURAL REFERENCE... ISSUES... HOPES... SENSE OF MORALITY. IN ARCHITECTURE... WE USE TECHNOLOGY... WE DON'T USE CULTURAL UNDERSTANDING

It has taken us a long time to change the nature of the means. Surely ideas can be encapsulated in different ways because we have the ability to collate the data in a different manner? So we essentially have put the blocks on certain types of things, so that notion of acceptance of change and difference, those notions of individuality are suppressed. That repression produces a whole series of issues, in fact you could argue that some forms of contemporary art such as rap or graffiti are, I suppose, those few rare moments when the steam escapes from the vessel. The question is then what does this teach us? It is about the expression of an idea at its most direct. I would argue that rap is in many ways an echo of a street opera that has existed from the seventeenth century onwards and this notion also parallels itself with Kabuki and Noh. Kabuki the common and Noh the exalted. This is in a sense the nature

kind of circumstance, and what we do with that is we use technology to drive it, we don't use cultural understanding.

The interesting thing about current popular music is that the first thing is that it is understandable, the second is that it has a message and the third is that it uses mixed media, so there is the tune, the beat which everyone can join in, there is the message and its articulacy and then there is the song. They combine together with the performance to render a kind of authenticity which you can embrace to some extent. Architecture has exactly the same possibility; this thing of form following the function began to give us spaces which are de-culturalised, they are not about a specific group of people wanting to re-set their version of material, form and status. We seem to forget the underlying reasons for half of these things, and so, when we look at the way we teach students we forget the reasons why students tend to produce all sort of the same thing, that some things are right and some things are wrong. Far more interesting are the attempts by some places to follow an investigation, an investigation of a phenomenon, and these things are 'kind of' definable by observation and you've learnt enough of them that you are able to give it a name, so we are going back to the question of how you create a taxonomy, how you collate things. But what I say is that perhaps there is another way of using that notion of phenomena, and that may well be 'I am not simply going "I have observed x, y, z, b, and g, and they tell me certain things in a certain order"', it is asking 'what are the possibilities in relation to the observable phenomena?' It means that students from all sorts of backgrounds and all sorts of disciplines can become involved in the big game – which is the remaking of the environment – they have something to contribute that is

future cities and maybe even the cities we don't have on this planet.

EE *So what role might the tutor or advisor or guider have in that? Maybe Ray Land's 'threshold concept' is quite helpful to use as a way in, which explains the moment of transformation that takes place in an individual through learning, from which there is no return; your state of being is irreversibly altered. Interestingly, the focus is usually the transformation of the student as led by the tutor. Do you think that perhaps this idea could be taken beyond a student's understanding of the subject matter being studied and its implications, to an educator's own understanding of the heart of the subject? By doing that, the transformation of that subject through shared dialogues would have to be acknowledged. We are always focusing on the student and it is a way of saying well actually there is a shared relationship in this transformative experience, one is not led by 'other'.*

STUDENTS FROM ALL SORTS OF BACKGROUNDS AND DISCIPLINES CAN BECOME INVOLVED IN THE BIG GAME – THE REMAKING OF THE ENVIRONMENT – THEY HAVE SOMETHING TO CONTRIBUTE THAT IS VALUABLE

valuable because their experiences are now valuable. That's where I think the future gain in architecture can be and should, and I think that will make and very different sorts of places will begin to change the kind of configuration of our cities and our

LR It is quite interesting how many people say 'well I am not a teacher, I am a lecturer' – meaning they want someone to enshrine their status, when I think that there is a position as a facilitator. What does that mean? A student has no tools. You can assist them in acquiring tools, in making tools, you can assist them by giving them a sense of what was before if that is what they would like to do because there may be a useful lesson to be learnt in it. Quite often what we do is present work and say 'this is good work' and explain how we believe that work has come into being. We offer the student a system by which they may develop and produce that, like Eisenman's PhD which diagrammises how to produce Corbusian architecture, the meaning of the piloti, all of the elements, and how through a series of constructs they begin to orchestrate an order, not unlike the classical orders of architecture and how they are used.

EE *And that is an instruction.*

LR Exactly. And that seems to me to be where many students become lost in a process of attempting to live up to or to replicate that which they don't really understand. Because they don't really understand the means or the purposes or the function, there is no attempt to redefine the nature of the function, or question it. We are up against the one immutable thing – time. But what we could do is express an interesting experiment that took all the time we had available and immersed ourselves in learning, or working with, or adding to, a new kind of canon, and the canon is about tools of investigation and tools of production. We may think we are already doing it but in many ways all we are doing is replicating buildings and replicating the things we think that people will like. In conversation with a partner

of a significant British practice, he, and it would be a he, even today, said, "do you know, my frustration is that you get these young people come in and they don't know how to do anything, they have no idea, they come up with these drawings and they are meaningless". The reason that those 'young people' produce work in that way is because they are caught between two interesting worlds. That production is a filter which separates them from an 'other' group of students who might well be interested in the production of something and how it comes together and its meaning and its evaluation, but the tutors believe that this 'other' way, this form of directed experiment, is the next step in a continuing movement to complicate the means of production. We have almost a priesthood of what is worthy and what is not. It is quite extraordinary.

EE *If I have understood you correctly, there are students that go and work in offices that don't understand the work they have done at university because they have been 'instructed' and then there is a situation where the students might produce something that the partner in practice does not understand, because maybe the student has been true to themselves, certain of their identity, in that production. This is what we were earlier alluding to as a better future, where education is more about mentoring both ways, about learning and recognising individuality as opposed to simply favouring the favoured. So, in relation to that, there is a question around the issue in architecture education where* architecture is part of the reality of the built environment, part of the future of our built environment, but we are educating for this industry, an industry that cannot really accommodate either of those types of educated architect; whether that is the extreme of the student not understanding the work they are presenting or the partner not understanding the work of the student.

LR Yes, but remember the practices are based in a very old binary notion of what architecture is meant to be, beginning with the fact that architecture practices produce 10% of what is created in the world, so they have a very specific understanding; the buildings they have learnt to do are correct and as we are in a reductionist development of more buildings, that's what we do. We have technology that deals with the issues that we need to solve. But we have climate change which is making some of that untenable, we have cost which is making some of that untenable, nonetheless those people still have

EE So I wonder what you think that we as educators, or facilitators, do? Do we hope that we can change industry, or do we accept that we are providing for their economic situation of perpetuating practice? Do we have a chance? Do you think there is a role we can play?

LR Is there a difference? Between being an educator and being in practice? I don't think there is a difference, I think that architecture, this mother of the arts, by definition embraces everything and now in a time where buildings don't have to exist for you to encounter them it is important to be aware of everything from parametrics, to film, to video to SFX. All of these things are enablers of environments so that people can live and thrive – thrive being a key word. The notion of thriving is really important, so what do we do about that, maybe we do a version of what some regimes do. Is it possible for us to de-educate ourselves? To go through a series of scenarios

IS IT POSSIBLE FOR US TO DE-EDUCATE OURSELVES? TO GO THROUGH A SERIES OF SCENARIOS WHICH ALLOW US TO DE-COLONISE OUR THINKING?

very traditional views about who and what an architect should be and what they should be involved in. This same partner said to me "you train these people and they go out and do films". Ok. Some people would agree that an architect shouldn't do films. I say, why shouldn't a film maker do architecture?

which allow us to de-colonise our thinking? Is that important? I think it is important because without that we will continue to produce 'capital' which is less than worthy and will hold back many of the really useful creative notions that exist amongst students. We should look at different ways of delivering. We could look at the music industry and the way in which it is democratised by the use of technology. We should look at different forms of engagement that allow ideas and thoughts – concepts – to be given space, to have meaning. And that's what I mean by poly-culture – a series of different kinds of cultural understandings that one can value and consider. Not having to merge as in multi-culture, where you are unsure of what is what.

EE *You talk about responsive participants – and I think that is a helpful way of putting it, it implies a relationship or dialogue rather than one over-ruling another. Then you have brought up creativity which, interestingly, when other people talk about architecture or when business talks about what it can learn from architecture, or what they need, it is always innovation and creativity; but*

EE *And so actually, as architecture educators or facilitators, many of us are working in a really culturally diverse situation. We have a responsibility to nurture the idea of what Paulo Freire calls a 'critical consciousness'; as something that comes out of a dialogue and relies on an engagement in a type of praxis which has its origins in clear response to acute awareness of a type of oppression. Political or racial, but actually also in terms of creative oppression – an oppression of being an 'object' of others' will rather than a self-determining 'subject'.*

LR Jean-Jacques Rousseau has stuff to say on this, it is not new. Franz Fanon has a whole host of stuff to say on this, and James Baldwin's kind of, I suppose, veiled ramblings about love, emotion and justifications have loads to say about these things, and that's why I think the notion of the building,

WHERE WISDOM IS IMPOSED ON THE 'CREATOR' BY 'OTHER', IT IS STIFLING AND WHERE IT IS SELF-GENERATED, CREATIVITY FLOURISHES

within architecture itself it is a bit of a taboo sometimes. There is an idea elsewhere that creativity and wisdom are intrinsically linked. But where wisdom is imposed on the 'creator' by 'other', it is stifling, and where is it self-generated, creativity flourishes. I think that is implicit in what you have just described, as a way of being what could be described as polyamorous in education!

LR Yes yes yes!

when you walk through Paris, post-Haussmann, you are seeing truly the vision of an empire writ entirely in a language it believes it has taken and enriched and surpassed. It eradicates its mediaeval past as being too much like 'others' and begins to describe itself.

EE *Which comes back again to what you were saying about certainty of self and confidence in that communication and, undeniably in a way, whether*

*one agrees with what is being said
in an opera or a rap or what's being
communicated through urban design
or architecture, it is undeniably
impressive and moves one almost just
because of its certainty. So I guess there
is a nice idea that if everyone could
have more self-certainty we might have
more varied 'wows'.*

LR We have some groups that thrive
and some that don't. I would wish
to see all groups thriving, sharing
those things which they experience
alongside having a real understanding
of how the development of historical
products has happened and its
meaning. Then there is a ground we
can play with. Is it too complex for
someone to teach? I mean, we could
teach history and theory thematically,
in the context of socio-economic
drivers at any time which explain it,
and that makes a big difference. If
you don't, it means some people are
constantly excluded from the picture.

EE *I wonder whether maybe if we
acknowledge the impossibility of
solving this issue with current leaders,
we can still go some way to enabling
a response or change. If not, we are in
a difficult situation. So, for example,
a truly inclusive curriculum and
pedagogic approach is in fact a fantasy,
but that knowledge of it as fantasy
becomes crucial in driving the cultural
changes and shifts we are looking for.*

LR You are referring to theory of the
impossibility of change and I get that
and I understand absolutely that we
can identify it but we cannot do very
much about it, and so here comes the

McPherson report and institutional
racism. So everyone finds the word
racism painful. I am not quite sure
why, I mean, you kind of like what
you know, but you know you should
like that which is of value to you or to
society. You know that you should not
judge in advance because you have
no idea of the outcome. You know that
the society we live in is essentially
established on the basis of lots of
effort and input from 'other' and that
continues today. We make decisions
which seem to suggest that we have
an innate racial complex that excludes
'others' because they don't wish to
adapt to what we or you have. I think it
is important to bring that to the table
and that if we begin to discuss those
complex issues and we once again
re-address the nature of ownership of
different kinds of cultural strands, we
begin to see that we share a warp and
weft of material – the cultural outputs
of this planet – and then we are in
a much better position to value and
understand how those came to be, and
then we have dialogue.

EE *Dialogue is an important part
because there is a sense in some places
that if you simply put enough different
people in the room it will solve the
problem, but it doesn't necessarily.*

LR For me the real problem is around
need. Whilst we in the West need
labour, with an aging population
we are going to need young people
from other places. We could support
people in other places directly and at
the same time borrow temporarily
their skills while we go through this
transition. That exchange would

mean, say, not simply taking doctors away from the Indian subcontinent, but exchanging that with new technologies we have available, whilst coming to some sort of critical understanding of the value of both groups, rather than saying 'they have taken our jobs'. These conundrums are exhausting, and they are not tenable, there will have to be a shift. Why? Because the 'third world' is rapidly becoming a 'first world'. Singapore

of change that we are living through which we can participate in?

LR   Like the second world war? Where they destroyed so much, they had to build even more bad stuff to replace it!

EE   *Before we met today, I was wondering whether we were going to end up by concluding that we are still in the same situation of endless repetition – like 'Institute Benjamenta'*

ARCHITECTS SHOULD... SEE THEMSELVES AS SOCIAL INTERVENTIONISTS... TO READ SOCIETY, TO PRODUCE FOR SOCIETY RE-READINGS OF WHAT IT CAN AND COULD BE

is the first country who set a 30-year agenda and has achieved it. It is a 'first world' nation. Malaysia is next on the list. So things are changing.

EE   *So how do we bring this back to the question of architecture education?*

LR   I think that we have to realise that in our understandings of the hegemony of western cultural construct that those days are gone. What we have is a Disneyland of things we once thought were great. They have served their purpose and we will keep some, but some will have to go. We will adapt many but new notions of living and experience mean that people have changed their requirements. The constructs we are delivering are essentially outmoded.

EE   *So do you feel like this is a positive moment in the sense that it is a moment*

– or whether we were going to end up feeling positive and optimistic, saying actually there is a potential for it not to be like that anymore because there are various, albeit sometimes superficial, but nonetheless present energies pushing for a change.

LR   Architects spend most of their time trying to get jobs where they produce more of the same in order to solve a problem of accommodation when they haven't rethought what that accommodation problem is. They respond to their clients in that way, they see themselves as servants, but servants with an ego. The building skin is now their representation of ego. Architects should really see themselves as social interventionists and in that sense their job is to read society, to produce for society re-readings of what it can and could be, and to offer those as possibilities to solve or to negotiate the territory between need and want.

EE *There are people who think that architects should not be sociologists or politicians, but I share your approach and believe we have a role to play as thinkers in all of this. Sociology, philosophy and psychology don't play a part in most curriculum, a massive omission.*

LR You should teach contextual history in terms of these themes, so people understand the product. A thematic understanding of the production of buildings, or culture, helps to deal with how a building affects the populous; simply by opening or closing its doors, simply by existing, it talks about your status in the world. I think that is part of the

areas of the world which have issues with shelter and climate change. What is the code? Increasingly, many of our ideas and images are redundant. How are we going to get these new ones to happen? Are we going to still constantly talk about building typologies that have been around for centuries, like the library of Alexandria? We are in a world where I keep more information on my mobile phone, I have access to much more than any library could have, and that means that people who live in situations which otherwise would be considered to be poor or poverty-driven have as much information as I do; so the equalities have changed. We don't teach our students that.

EE *Knowledge equalities have changed and then the point of knowledge being*

A THEMATIC UNDERSTANDING OF THE PRODUCTION OF BUILDINGS, OR CULTURE, HELPS TO DEAL WITH HOW A BUILDING AFFECTS THE POPULOUS

whole socially-engineered conundrum – because it is not that simple – that we have to unpick, that we have to find a way of unpicking. The other thing is that if we look at architecture as being a social and a commercial construct, and we look at architects as being part of the facilitators of those things, they have to understand the impact of their work and how that work translates into social conditioning. We know these things, we know the symbols, we know their meanings: it's a code. But what is the code that we need for when we move beyond the boundaries of our planet and what is the code for those

combined with creativity and the relevance of where that knowledge comes from has to be opened up in order to move forward.

LR And we are back to the old men who run institutions. Can they change? Everybody changes when they are in a situation that warrants change.

EE *When it benefits them to change.*

LR When it benefits them, or their survival. Where it allows them to get some kind of sense of being on the ascendency, and it is clear that, now, it is about knowledge.

EE *So to go back to the title of this 'dialogue' – conscientização – 'conscientisation' in English, raising consciousness' or developing a 'critical*

difference to the way in which we deal with other people. It's language language language. Language, culture behaviour. Language, cultural behaviour, openness. Embracing. It's about those sorts of things and it's about also an absolute understanding

WE BELIEVE THAT BECAUSE THEY SOUND DIFFERENT, THEIR THINKING IS DEFECTIVE. WE DON'T VALUE THEIR THINKING OR EXPLORE WHAT IT MIGHT MEAN

consciousness'. If there is a push for, or an already existing opportunity for, information to be accessed by 'all', then this idea of 'raising consciousness' is one of the key things that could challenge the block, the unwillingness to change.

LR I think you have to have plural accesses to information, and I think one of the things that we, that I, have glossed over is the fundamental notion of how we deal with 'other', because 'other' isn't simply about race, it is also about class, and I think that it is very easy to identify when it comes to race, but we still do nothing about it. We are quite content to have students come into the academy and fail them. We fail them because we believe they have been given a privilege; we don't believe that they necessarily have a right. We believe that they don't have the capability to perform at a high level and we slot them into a set position. We believe that because they sound different, their thinking is defective. We don't value their thinking or explore what their thinking might mean. These are the key things which make a

of one's own ignorance, and our need to know in order to develop. Artificial Intelligence has its drawbacks because it learns from what it takes in and on that basis it would then, if it had to choose people to enter universities, it would mitigate against women because they don't appear in as much literature as men, there are more negative comments about women in literature than there are about men, and so it would do a sorting exercise which would begin to push women out. But, nonetheless, when it comes to analysis of data on matter, it suddenly found new antibiotics. It searches indiscriminately for trace elements that could be used to fight a range of diseases which currently are drug resistant. What it has done is put things together to see what they do, and every so often it finds one!

EE *So if it is searching through something which is seemingly unknown and doesn't have a history, then it is going to find something new, whereas if it is searching through literature or previously input information it is going to reinforce those norms.*

LR Yes, because it deals with the data that has been accumulated by white men.

EE *But how is that going to be challenged?*

LR That is my point. That is exactly my point about poly-culture. There are other cultures and cultural references which have existed over a similar time-frame or longer, but they are not documented in the same way, perhaps, and then also the notion of cultural appropriation is not explicit. These things are really important to delight in investigation and to re-search again, to find out what things really are and where they come from.

EE *As Paulo Friere put it: to be conscious is to be conscious of being. It is interesting that they call it 'artificial intelligence' not 'artificial consciousness'.*

LR Yes, that is true.

of problems that we face as designers. We don't see ourselves in those terms. We are about differentiation not commonalities, and in fact architectural teaching is about saying some things are good and some things are bad and not trying to make the best of all qualities 'in lak'ech ala k'in': 'I am another you, you are another me'.

EE *That explains so much to have a culture or a language where in just a few words so much is embodied, as opposed to our 'hello' which has origins as being more of a command for the 'other' to stop and listen, 'how are you?' which places the onus on 'other'.*

LR 'Namaste': I bow to the greatness that is in you; those kinds of greetings don't exist in the West and that is what predicates our education system, because our education systems is religious and therefore hierarchical by definition. That is the fundamental of what we are talking about today, all of these attitudes, and

THE MAYAN GREETING... 'IN LAK'ECH ALA K'IN'... 'I AM ANOTHER YOU, YOU ARE ANOTHER ME'... A VERY IMPORTANT POINT OF REFERENCE FOR ALL OF US

EE *And to have 'artificial consciousness' you would have to have 'empathy'.*

LR That is crucial. The Mayan greeting 'in lak'ech' – 'I am another you' is a very important point of reference for all of us. It may seem a little bit romantic, but it is very useful in describing why we have the sorts

it is also the suppression of, or the re-categorisation of, other kinds of cultural production around that core.

EE *So that is what has to be re-invented?*

LR Yes because we are not in that time any longer. Even though we still wear the gowns.

Liverpool School of Architecture // RIBA Education Debate
Wednesday 11 April 2018

In August 2017, the RIBA education review published 'bold aims' for the future of architectural education. Seven months on, in the context of Brexit and a continuously changing higher education environment, the Liverpool School of Architecture hosted a debate that brought together the RIBA and architectural educators from across the region to discuss how the sector might respond to the future challenges and opportunities. Each guest was invited to present a 'position statement' as a provocation for the debate. This event was filmed and can be viewed at:
https://www.liverpool.ac.uk/architecture/news/stories/title,1045906,en.html

Guests:
Soumyen Bandyopadhyay *Stirling Chair in Architecture, University of Liverpool*
Prue Chiles *Professor of Architectural Design Research and Acting Director of Architecture, Newcastle University School of Architecture Planning and Landscape*
Ben Derbyshire *President, RIBA*
Alex Dusterloh *Director of Studies, University of Liverpool*
Elantha Evans *Senior Lecturer, School of Architecture + Cities, University of Westminster*
Rosa Urbano Gutierrez *Associate Professor, University of Liverpool*
Rob Hyde *Senior Lecturer, Manchester School of Architecture*
Daniel Jary *Head of Teaching and Learning, School of Architecture, University of Sheffield*
Alan Jones *Vice President for Education, RIBA*
Colin Pugh *PSRB Lead, Manchester School of Architecture, Secretary to SCHOSA*
Ola Uduku *Professor, Manchester School of Architecture*
Dominic Wilkinson *Senior Lecturer, Liverpool School of Art and Design LJMU*

EPILOGUE
FROM THIRDSPACE TO TERTIARY PLACE
A VITAL 'OTHER' FOR THE UNIVERSITY

EE For a few minutes, consider how you see the different practices of architecture, its training, and its perception by the industry and wider world within which it sits. What do we do, how do we do it, and when? Are our processes and products design-led, commercially-driven or professional services to be slotted in within a chosen procurement route?

To produce a building, how long do we think for, draw for, talk for?

It is well acknowledged, and likely a main part of the foundation for this debate, that the variety of encouraged architecture practices at university often differ from the experienced ways of working in industry – what is taught, or learnt, may not align with what is done in the office. Indeed, these are often pitched as binary, one against the other. But perhaps more importantly, we could ask, what the similarities are? Where do they lie and why are they important?

So, rather than placing practice and academia as irreconcilable opposites, what we should be doing, in education – as architects and educators – is developing a new, clearer and more self-sustainable position for the profession of architecture, to clarify its definition, for itself as a discipline and for what impact it has on the built environment.

In response to the RIBA Education Review, we should consider more carefully what role the university could have in this.

The relationship between architectural practice and education is tightened in the Education Review, with 'industry and professionalism having a closer and more leading role in both curriculum content and delivery'. It is possibly worth noting that 'industry', the 'profession' and 'practice' are not interchangeable words.

In the UK, architectural education, as we know it, was invented by working professionals as something 'outside' the profession, with the AA set up in 1847 as a critical, supportive forum for enquiry and reflection outside the architects' working lives and beyond an apprenticeship-type training. Later, architectural education was housed in universities – communities of teachers and scholars – and in polytechnics which, in principle, offered a more vocational and technical training.

How much of the RIBA's work is now in mediating between industry, practice and education; an attempt to declare a common ground or a practice for all; to lobby government groups and to provide guidance? Diversity in academic approaches is both acclaimed and restrained simultaneously – a decree that we must export our services, join in the big business rush in China AND at the same time diversify into smaller, 'alternative practices'. Are we hedging our bets, or spreading ourselves thinly?

Recently, there has been much talk of the 'value' of the architect across these spectrums – exposed through an accolade of awards for final products – but there is little clarification of what that value actually is, beyond applying 'good design' or how its qualities are nurtured, what in our practices enable 'it' to happen, or what impact might the Education Review or Brexit have on 'it'.

Is our value in a skills base? In innovative thinking? In visionary ideas? Creativity? In using our ability to synthesise information and in problem solving? Perhaps we, as a profession, need to define what we are 'training' for and how we think our value is best offered to the 'industry', rather than being led by it? With the RIBA addressing the bigger questions, how can the university more precisely interrogate questions around delivery – both of architecture education and of buildings?

I am reading a book at the moment by Edward Soja called *Thirdspace* and perhaps it helps us here, in that its central argument is that spatial thinking has tended to be presented as either concrete material (or we could say, the process of building and its physical product) which can be tangibly mapped or analysed; or as mental constructs (ideas, representations and meanings or social significances). In our architectural practices, we can see that under current extreme pressures, mental and physical processes may be converging, but they do still need each other as distinct entities and require a discursive relationship to be of use.

Soja proposes an alternative approach that comprehends both the material and the mental dimensions of spatiality, but which moves them into a different mode of thinking.

To quote:

> In what I call a critical strategy of 'thirding-as-othering', I try to open up our spatial imaginaries to ways of thinking and acting politically that respond to all binarisms, to any attempt to confine thought and political action to only two alternatives, by interjecting an 'Other' set of choices. In this critical 'thirding', the original binary choice is not dismissed entirely but is subjected to a creative process of restructuring that draws selectively and strategically from the two opposing categories to open up new alternatives.

So, if we accept a need for this 'critical thirding', what could or should the university's role be, as a 'third-space', and what can 'academics' do within that space to build a critical and enquiring dialogue with both practice and education?

Bhan, G. (2019). 'Notes on a Southern Urban Practice'. Environment and Urbanization 31(2), pp.639-654.

Blanchot, M. (1982). The Space of Literature. (A. Smock, Trans.). Lincoln, London: University of Nebraska Press.

Blanchot, M. & Foucault, M. (1990). Michel Foucault As I Imagine Him / Maurice Blanchot: The Thought from Outside. (B. Massumi & J. Mehlman, Trans.). New York: Zone Books.

Bo Bardi, L. (2013). Stones Against Diamonds. (A. Doyle & P. Johnston, Trans.) London: AA Publications.

Borch, C. (Ed.) (2014). Architectural Atmospheres: On the Experience and Politics of Architecture. Basel: Birkhauser.

Biesta, G.J.J. (2012). The Beautiful Risk of Education. London & New York: Routledge.

Brenan, G. (2012). The Spanish Labyrinth: The Social and Political Background of the Spanish Civil War. Cambridge: Cambridge University Press.

Calvino, I. (1997). Invisible Cities. (W. Weaver, Trans.). London: Vintage Books.

Collini, S. (2017) Speaking of Universities. London & New York: Verso.

Coverly, M. (2010). Psychogeography. Herts: Pocket Essentials.

Cullen, G. (1961). The Concise Townscape. New York: The Architectural Press (AP).

Evans, R. (1996). Translations from Drawing to Building and Other Essays. London: AA Documents.

Fanon, F. (2018) Alienation and Freedom. London: Bloomsbury Academic.

Friere, P. (2017). Pedagogy of the Oppressed. (M. Bergman Ramos, Trans.). London: Random House.

Hancox, D. (2013). The Village Against the World. London: Verso.

Gehl, J. (2008). The Life Between Buildings. Copenhagen: Danish Architectural Press.

Hill, J. (2006). Immaterial Architecture. New York: Routledge.

Hollis, E. (2010). The Secret Lifes of Buildings. London: Portobello Books.

Illich, I. (1986). H2O and the Waters of Forgetfulness. London: Marion Boyars.

Kahn, L. (1998). Conversations with Students. Rice: Princeton Architectural Press

Land, R. & Meyer, J.H.F. (2003). Threshold Concepts and Troublesome Knowledge. Oxford: Oxford Centre for Staff Development.

Leatherbarrow, D. (2009). *Architecture Oriented Otherwise*. New York: Princeton AP.

Lefebvre, H. (2004). *Rhythmanalysis: Space, Time and Everyday Life*. (S.Elden & G.Moore, Trans.). London: Bloomsbury.

Lynch, K. (1964). *The Image of a City*. Joint Venter for Urban Studies: MIT.

Montgomery, C. (2013) *Happy City: Transforming Our Lives through Urban Design*. Random House: Penguin.

Pallasmaa, J. (2012) *The Eyes of the Skin*. Chichester: Wiley.

Perec, G. (2008). *Species of Spaces and Other Pieces*. London: Penguin.

Rykwert, J. (1988). *The Idea of a Town*. London: Faber and Faber.

Sennett, R. (2003) *The Fall of the Public Man*. London: Penguin.

Sennett, R (2018). *The Craftsman*. London: Penguin.

Sennett, R. (2013). *Together*. London: Penguin.

Sinclair, I. (2003). *Lights out for the Territory*. London: Penguin.

Soja, E.W. (1998). *Thirdspace: Journeys to Los Angeles and other real-and-imagined places*. Oxford: Blackwell.

Strauven, F. (1998) *Aldo Van Eyck: The Shape of Relativity*. Amsterdam: Architectura & Natura.

Sudjic, D. (2011). *The Edifice Complex: The Architecture of Power*. London: Penguin.

Tindall, G. (2010). *The Fields Beneath: The history of one London Village*. London: Eland.

Wachsmuth, David (2014) 'City as Ideology: Reconciling the Explosion of the City Form with the Tenacity of the City Concept'. *Environment and Planning D: Society and Space* 32 (1): pp.75-90.

Walser, R. (1995) *Institute Benjamenta*. (C.Middleton, Trans.). Extraordinary Classics: Serpent's Tail.

Williams, R. (1988). *Keywords: A vocabulary of culture and society*. London: Fontana.

Whyte, W. H. (1980). *The Social life of Small Urban Spaces*. Project for Public Spaces.

BIBLIOGRAPHY

JASDEEP ATWAL completed her undergraduate degree in architecture, and has since been working as a freelance architectural assistant. She is returning to university in October this year to begin her MArch (RIBA part II) course in Architecture. Jasdeep's great love of calligraphy inspired her to open a shop – Artisan Moments – specialising in balloons, flowers and handmade gifts. Her ambition is to become a qualified architect and to set up a charity to support underprivileged countries build needed and appropriate housing for their communities.

SOUMYEN BANDYOPADHYAY is the Sir James Stirling Chair in Architecture at the Liverpool School of Architecture (LSA), having previously held professorial positions at the Manchester School of Architecture (MSA) and Nottingham Trent University. He directs the Centre for the Study of Architecture and Cultural Heritage of India, Arabia and the Maghreb (ArCHIAM), an interdisciplinary forum with research projects in Oman, Qatar, Morocco and India. Bandyopadhyay has extensive experience of architectural practice in India and the Middle East and has undertaken advisory and consultancy work in urban development, regeneration, architectural and urban design, and conservation.

VERONICA CAPPELLI has shifted from the realm of architecture design to concentrate on curation, exhibition design and writing in the museum sector and academia. Focusing on the early modern period, she has worked as a curatorial researcher in architectural history and authorship at the Royal Observatory, Greenwich. Veronica is about to start a Master's degree in Early Modern Studies to examine the geometries in Baroque architecture and their relationship with mathematical literature in Renaissance European and Sanskritic cultures. Once her arduous journey of ancient language learning is complete, she naïvely hopes to uncover all sacred texts concerning inhabited space to form a resolute opinion on the role architecture plays in language and culture preservation.

DUSAN DECERMIC is an architect and designer with extensive experience in practice and academia. He was for many years the Course Leader for MA Interiors at the University of Westminster and is currently co-leader of MArch studio DS11 'the intrinsic and extrinsic city'. In addition to a deep-rooted commitment to the importance of architecture in the city and for humankind, Dusan has a particular interest in exploring how the writings and theories of Jacques Lacan can support an experimental and reflective approach as part of the architecture design process.

ELANTHA EVANS is an architect and educator, currently co-leading MArch Design Studio DS11 with Dusan Decermic and working towards a PhD in architecture education. Projects carried out in practice as founding partner of Serrano Evans Partnership with Ana Serrano, included architecture, interior and object design, balanced with occasional site-specific performances and installations. Previous experience gained with Richard Rogers Partnership, Tim Ronalds Architects and Evans & Shalev was wide ranging, but consistently nurtured a clear design ethic holding the overall vision strong and following it through in the detail. From early on, Elantha's practice work was punctuated with design studio tutoring, first at HKU in 2000, later at Bath and then Westminster. A desire for a deeper understanding of the nature of architecture education and its institutional structures came with active involvement on RIBA Validation Panels in the UK & Overseas and was formalised further through completion of a PGcertHE and SFHEA membership. Following the completion of an MA in History & Critical Thinking at the Architectural Association in 2013, Elantha's creative endeavour shifted more fully into the realm of architecture education and research; first leading the BA year two design studio DS(2)01 at Westminster whilst also tutoring in MArch studio DS19, and now co-leading DS11 and acting as an external examiner at the University of Liverpool, Leicester DMU and UWL.

BIOGRAPHIES

CLARE HAMMAN studied architecture before gaining a Master's of Research in Cultural and Humanities Studies from the London Consortium, a collaborative programme composed of Birkbeck College, the Architectural Association, Institute of Contemporary Arts, and Tate Gallery. She now works as a designer, producer and film director, employing creative ways to represent history. Through critical analysis and representation of historical archives, she uses her multidisciplinary approach to create websites, films and books which convey narratives woven together by archive images and the written word.

ANDY LOWE was for many years a Lecturer and Architectural Theorist within the Department of Visual Cultures and the Centre for Research Architecture at Goldsmiths College, London. Andy studied at the University of Edinburgh and then at the Centre for Contemporary Studies at the University of Birmingham.

ANTHONY POWIS is an architect, researcher and design tutor. He worked at muf architecture/art between 2012 and 2017, focussing on public realm projects. He is currently completing a PhD – 'Thinking with Groundwater from Chennai' – as part of the Monsoon Assemblages research project funded by the European Research Council and based at the University of Westminster. He has been a design tutor in the BA Architecture programme since 2015 and now teaches a BA year two studio alongside Eric Guibert, with a focus on living systems design processes.

LAYTON REID is an architect, designer and educator. The founding Associate Dean for Architecture, Interior Design Environment Architectures and Urban Landscape Architecture at Ravensbourne University, London he developed a range of cross-disciplinary courses with an experimental, digital praxis, and a social-commercial ethos; encouraging access with a uniquely diverse student intake. Through Desitecture (a research-based design group), he considers and produces solutions for the design of cities and their construction. What are the future scenarios of the unasked questions? These visions are based on applied research in polyculture and the development of emergent technologies and materials; reconsidering the city as a responsive participant in society. Desitecture has presented, published and debated internationally. Layton is a champion of access to, and diversity in, architecture education and the liberation of the curriculum through internationalisation and the enfranchisement of the students' authentic contemporary experience of phenomena. He is currently creating a new diverse department of Architecture where he will continue to bring industrial and societal aspirations together to advance the development of relevant and inclusive studies in architecture and architecture design.

JOSHUA RICKETTS spent time working in the Fabrication Laboratory workshops at the University of Westminster and in practice for Pringle Richards Sharratt. Josh's experience ranges from model-making to conservation architecture and to wayfinding across a variety of projects. Combined with other collaborative projects such as this book and a pavilion for Helsinki design week 2019, these have helped to refocus and hone the unique contextualisation of each proposition during design development, an approach that will be developed further as part of his MArch (RIBA part II) studies later this year.

GADÉ SMITH was born and raised in south London, Since completing her undergraduate (RIBA part I) studies at the University of Westminster, she been working in the museum and exhibition design sector, as a 3D designer for Event, and workshop assistant for Collective Paper Aesthetics. In her spare time if she's not making dipped candles, she's creating ceramic holders for them and making other homeware objects such as decorative trays and side tables. This links to Gadé's interest in furniture design and she hopes to continue to work and collaborate in ways that combine these design fields and their different scales.

GIA SAN TU is a 'Part 1' architectural designer at the start-up practice ABHRA, working on private residential projects from RIBA Stage 1 to practical completion. As a result of her architectural history education in Italy, San naturally strives to put an emphasis on research and theory in her work. Returning to academia in September this year to pursue an MArch Architecture (RIBA part II), she would like to further explore the possibilities of 'intervention architecture' on historically significant buildings, maintaining an experimental and experiential approach to respond specifically to the needs of the building under examination.

The process of putting this book together has been immensely enjoyable, mainly due to the dedication and commitment of the editorial and production team: Jasdeep Atwal, Veronica Cappelli, Josh Ricketts, Gadé Smith and Gia San Tu. We met on Saturdays, every two weeks from September 2019 to January 2020 before entering an informal period of final editing. A group who started as ex-students of DS(2)01 from different years, are now friends and colleagues, to me and each other. I owe them many thanks and a lifetime of 'vino y tapas'. It was refreshing and enlightening to have this time together; collating, examining, discussing, selecting and presenting the work, images and words, to best communicate the projects and ideas. To have the opportunity to allow such in-depth, shared reflection on a wide-ranging body of student work is usually reserved for marking and moderation sessions, and is usually between tutors alone.

Many thanks also, of course, to all students of DS(2)01, whether their work is represented here or not. The ideal would have been full representation, but for a number of reasons this was not possible. Finishing touches have been completely dependant upon Josh Ricketts's tireless packaging, pedantry and patience with all of us, Guy Sinclair's scanning of crucial missing drawings, Clare Hamman's perpetual moral and technical support, and Charlotte Woodhead's pinpoint accuracy in editing. Special thanks also to the other contributors, to the students who participated in the reflections, to my supporters, friends and colleagues. To Andy Lowe for opening my mind to 'the outside', to Layton Reid for his unrelenting enthusiasm and desire to evolve ideas through dialogue, and of course most importantly to Anthony Powis and Dusan Decermic, my studio partners, without whom there would have been no DS(2)01 to write about. I am very grateful to Lindsay Bremner and Harry Charrington who had the foresight to develop this series and the trust to accept my proposal. Finally, thanks to our visiting critics, whose generous offer of time, support and critique has been invaluable to the students and the studio alike. 'Al pan pan y al vino vino'.

ACKNOWLEDGEMENTS

Dialogues and Dreams
DS[2]01: 2015-2018

Edited and compiled by Elantha Evans
With Jasdeep Atwal, Veronica Cappelli, Gia San-Tu, Gadé Smith and Joshua Ricketts

A University of Westminster, School of Architecture + Cities Publication

Book template designed by Mark Boyce

ISBN 978-0-9955893-6-0

The Studio as Book series are available to purchase at www.studioasbook.org

The editors have attempted to acknowledge all sources of images used and apologise for any errors or omissions.

School of Architecture + Cities
University of Westminster
35 Marylebone Road
London
NW1 5LS

Lightning Source UK Ltd.
Milton Keynes UK
UKHW050634271020
372303UK00003B/34